THE ILLUSION OF LIFE AND DEATH

MIND, CONSCIOUSNESS, AND ETERNAL BEING

CLARE GOLDSBERRY

FOREWORD BY RICHARD SMOLEY

Monkfish Book Publishing Company

Rhinebeck, New York

Paperback ISBN 978-1-948626-47-7
eBook ISBN 978-1-948626-48-4

Library of Congress Cataloging-in-Publication Data

Names: Goldsberry, Clare, 1947- author.
Title: The illusion of life and death : mind, consciousness, and eternal
    being / Clare Goldsberry ; foreword by Richard Smoley.
Description: Rhinebeck, New York : Monkfish Book Publishing Company, [2021]
    | Includes bibliographical references.
Identifiers: LCCN 2021025241 (print) | LCCN 2021025242 (ebook) | ISBN
    9781948626477 (paperback) | ISBN 9781948626484 (ebook)
Subjects: LCSH: Life. | Death. | Life--Religious aspects. |
    Death--Religious aspects.
Classification: LCC BD431 .G525 2021 (print) | LCC BD431 (ebook) | DDC
    128--dc23
LC record available at https://lccn.loc.gov/2021025241
LC ebook record available at https://lccn.loc.gov/2021025242

Book and cover design by Colin Rolfe
Cover painting: "New York" (1911) by George Bellows

Monkfish Book Publishing Company
22 East Market Street, Suite 304
Rhinebeck, NY 12572
(845) 876-4861
monkfishpublishing.com

THE ILLUSION OF LIFE AND DEATH

To Brent W. Deupree, my soulmate,
who taught me how to live
and, more importantly, how to die

CONTENTS

Foreword

by RICHARD SMOLEY

There is, to my knowledge, no book entitled *The Joy of Dying*, but many come close. There are *The Joy in Dying* by T Sky, *Joy in the Journey* by Sharol Hayner, and Steve Hayner and *Living While Dying* by Donna Tarrant.

How can these authors speak with authority? Unless you accept the doctrine of reincarnation, no one has actually experienced death. Even if we have lived and died in past lives, we generally do not remember them. The near-death experience, as its name indicates, may be close to death but is not death itself.

This fact leads me to wonder about the expertise of these authors. After all, if I buy a book called *The Joy of Plumbing*, I expect it to be written by someone who has a great deal of experience with wrenches and pipes. Some certainly see death and its effects more often and immediately than most—hospice nurses, undertakers—but ultimately they are like the rest of us: they have not died themselves.

Such titles indicate a glibness about death in modern American society, which masks a profound discomfort with this most ultimate of subjects. Do people fear death? At any rate, they fear thinking about it. This is evident in coverage of every major disaster: sudden and unexpected loss of life is treated as the worst thing that can possibly happen.

Past generations faced death very differently. In the first place, it was in plain view. People died at home, and they were often waked at home as well. Many of the nineteenth-century brownstone houses of Brooklyn, New York, have niches in their narrow stairwells called coffin rests, which enabled the resident family to fit a coffin through as they moved it down the stairs. In the same era, it was common to photograph the deceased in an open casket along with the survivors, often in their living room. Today most people would regard this as a gross violation of taste.

Much of the immediacy of death in earlier times had to do with poverty. A new widow might barely have been able to afford even the expense of a coffin and a meal for the guests and often had no clear idea where the next week's money would come from, so there was no question of shipping the body off to a costly funeral director. But there was also the presence of religion—and because I am talking about America, this was Christianity, the nation's dominant faith.

From its inception, Christianity has always been intimately preoccupied with death. In *Doctor Zhivago,* Boris Pasternak writes, "Art has two constant, two unending concerns: it always meditates on death and thus always creates life. All great, genuine art resembles and continues the Revelation of St. John."

Christian art has indeed meditated constantly on death. Sometimes these images can be gruesome. Anyone who has visited medieval cathedrals in Europe will have seen the sepulchers of noblemen and bishops. Usually they are in full regalia—armor or ecclesiastical vestments. One exception was Paul Bush, the first bishop of Bristol, England, in the sixteenth century. His sepulcher, on display in Bristol Cathedral, has a stone effigy of him portrayed as a half-rotted corpse. Evidently Bishop Bush wanted to drive home the message of the mortality of the flesh particularly vividly.

Like many such representations, a gravestone carving found in Boston's Colonial cemetery sends a double message. A skull and crossbones points to the body's demise. But the skull also has a pair of wings, alluding to the invisible soul that flies off to the afterlife. An image like this one signifies that death, though *an* end, is not *the* end; not only is there a reality beyond, but that reality, being eternal, is far more significant than the few decades of an uncertain and often painful life on earth. As such, awareness of death must be kept ever-present in the foreground.

This idea is still alive in the monastic tradition. As Clare Goldsberry notes in this book, the Benedictine monk David Steindl-Rast writes that at the monastery, monks are "counseled (or challenged) to have death at all times before our eyes."

Traditional Catholicism speaks of the *quattuor novissima*, the "Four Last Things": Death, Judgment, Heaven, and Hell. These stages of the end of life and the afterlife were brought vividly before believers' eyes, and a vast body of literature—and practice—dealt with preparation for these "last things." In *The Rule and Exercise of Holy Denying*, the seventeenth-century English divine Jeremy Taylor writes: "He that will die well and happily must dress his Soul by a diligent and frequent scrutiny: he must perfectly understand and watch the state of his Soul; he must set his house in order before he is fit to die. And for this there is great reason, and great necessity."

The practice of the *buen morir*, "the good death," a time of penitence and contemplation before an anticipated death, was aimed at putting the house of the soul in order. This may have been done by the most powerful monarch of the sixteenth century, the Holy Roman Emperor Charles V. In 1556, he turned over his holdings in Austria and Germany to one son; in 1558, shortly before his death, he handed the throne of Spain to another. Although matters of state no doubt played a part, it was widely believed that his abdication was motivated by his desire for the *buen morir*. Ignatius Loyola, founder of the Jesuit order, writes, "The emperor gave a rare example to his successors...in so doing, he proved himself to be a true Christian prince...may the Lord in all His goodness now grant the emperor freedom."

Today these certainties have eroded, though most Americans

still believe in the afterlife. According to a 2017 survey by one polling source, Rasmussen Reports, "62% of American Adults believe in life after death. Just 17% do not, but 20% are still unsure if there's an afterlife." This seems plausible: sixty-two percent (five eighths) of the population have some arguably clear concept of life after death; the rest are either agnostic or don't believe in the afterlife at all.

Apparently, beliefs in the afterlife—even if they remain strong—are much vaguer than they were a hundred years ago. Or, rather, people feel freer to voice their uncertainties than they did when conventional religion held a firmer grasp.

Despite the much-publicized "denial of death" (the title of a bestseller by Ernest Becker that won the Pulitzer Prize in 1974), Americans are probably franker and more open in discussing this subject than they were two or three generations ago. In the 1960s, when I was a boy, it was still common practice for a doctor diagnosing cancer to tell the family rather than the patient, who, it was felt, needed to be shielded from this calamity.

That is what happened to my mother: at one point, her mother's gynecologist told her that he thought my grandmother had cancer. My mother spent ten days in anguish about this possibility before the doctor changed his mind (my grandmother would live for almost another twenty years). In this case, perhaps the old practice had some wisdom to it, although it would have been better still if the doctor had kept his mouth shut and not told anybody anything.

These considerations lead us to the present work. Clare Goldsberry's book is a skillful, learned, and heartfelt exploration of death from a religious, philosophical, and personal standpoint, interweaving the teachings of the world's great traditions with her story of accompanying her partner, Brent, in his eighteen-month struggle with esophageal cancer. Brent, she tells us, achieved a present-day version of the *buen morir*, "dying quietly, peacefully, without fear, and free from attachments either to the body or to others."

Goldsberry's account gives a vivid and precise idea, not necessarily of how everyone should face death, but of how one man did so with courage and integrity. Whether we ourselves will be able to follow his example when our time comes is an open question, but I believe that we can draw a great deal of knowledge and inspiration from Brent's (and Goldsberry's) story.

Goldsberry elaborates in enlightening detail on Hindu and Buddhist concepts of the Self and its relation to life and death. Without wishing to put words in her mouth, this is how I understand them: As she indicates, we continually identify ourselves with the body. Most people feel this way most of the time, and this attitude has been given intellectual reputability by the widespread (but unproven and indeed false) doctrine that the mind and Self are merely the side effects of brain processes. When these processes cease, so do the Self and personal identity; that may be too bad, but that is how it is, and we may as well just accept it.

Problems with this doctrine are rife, and it has not been aided by the voluminous reports of near-death experiences over the past half century, in which, despite the assertions of science, patients obstinately keep having experiences—often profound, beautiful, and insightful ones—when their brain waves had ceased.

In short, death certainly involves the physical body, but the physical body is not the totality. What is left? The soul, perhaps. But it would be easier to explain the theory of relativity to your dog than it would be to get a clear answer from current religion about what the soul is.

In the New Testament, *soul* is invariably a translation of the Greek *psukhé*: psyche. This fact makes it all much easier to understand. The soul is the psyche—the complex of thoughts, emotions, images, and memories, conscious and unconscious—that make up personal identity.

Is this soul immortal? It seems unlikely. Part of this psyche is universal and collective (the archetypes of Jung), and part of it is the result of individual conditioning and experience. How much of this is likely to survive death? You may identify intensely with your political beliefs, but will you be a Republican or a Democrat after you are dead? The very question is ridiculous. Even your religion may not matter as much as you think.

The esoteric traditions generally see the situation this way: this soul, this psyche, does in fact survive physical death—but for a short time only, perhaps around forty days. Tibetan lamas, for example, read the *Bardo Thödol*, known as the Tibetan Book of Dead, to the departed person for forty-nine days after death.

What then? This soul, this psyche, often known in the esoteric traditions as the *astral body*, dies too. It dissipates into its constituent elements just as the physical body does.

These reflections grow disturbing. We may be able to cope with the fact that we are going to be separated from our fleshly forms, but our psyches—are they not *us*? If they go, what is left?

The traditional teaching, again, is that something survives even the death of the body and psyche. In esoteric Christianity, it was called the *spirit* (as opposed to the soul; originally the two were rigorously distinguished); Hinduism calls it the *atman*; other religions have other names for it. This is what survives; this is what is immortal.

Put in the simplest possible terms, this spirit, this atman, is what in you says *I*. You may think you are your thoughts, emotions, opinions, but as you can easily see in certain simple meditative practices, you can step back from all of these and watch them as if they were on a screen. They are quite distinct from this "I," this Self, which can watch all these events of one's life, inner and outer, as if they belonged to someone else.

This is the Self that is immortal. You can never see it, because it is always that which sees, but you can never lose it either. Strictly speaking, it is not God, but it is the place in us from which we connect with God. If you prefer to use the Hindu terms *Advaita Brahma*, this is why atman and Brahman are one.

We could even say that the real objective of life is to realize this truth, not only conceptually but experientially. To do so is to achieve the *buen morir*, whether it occurs on the deathbed or decades before. If we are to trust scriptures like the *Tibetan Book of the Dead*, we can realize this identify after death as well.

In his book *The Master Game*,[1] Robert S. de Ropp, a

---

[1] de Ropp, Robert S. *The Master Game: Pathways to Higher Consciousness*. Nevada City, CA: Gateways Books & Tapes, 2003.

physician and teacher of the Gurdjieff-Ouspensky tradition, remarks:

> The "art of intentional dying" has nothing to do with *personal survival* after death. It involves rather a reblending of the separate consciousness with a larger, more generalized state that may be thought of as all-pervading. In the language of Tantric Buddhism, this state is called the *dharma-kaya*, and reentry into the *dharma-kaya* through the condition known as Clear Light is what the master of yoga achieves at death.

These comments tell us that life after death is more than a matter of the survival of the little self (however unsettling that thought may be). It is, rather, the integration of the smaller identity into a larger one.

Is this a reassuring conclusion or a disturbing one? Even at this level of union with the All, does the individual survive in some form? I cannot answer, but I suspect that you will not reach this level until personal survival is a matter of utter indifference to you.

—RICHARD SMOLEY
Winfield, Illinois
July 2020

Richard Smoley is editor of *Quest: Journal of the Theosophical Society in America*. His twelve books include *Inner Christianity: A Guide to the Esoteric Tradition, Forbidden Faith: The Secret History of Gnosticism*, and *The Dice Game of Shiva: How*

Consciousness Creates the Universe. His latest book, *The Truth about Magic,* was published by G&D Media in February 2021.

Introduction

WHAT IS DEATH?

The *Asclepius* is a text that is part of a larger series called the *Corpus Hermeticum*, the "Hermetic body" of works dating back to late antiquity. It is a dialogue between the divine Hermes Trismegistus and his pupil Asclepius. When questioned about death, Hermes replies:

> For death occurs, which is the dissolution of the labors of the body and the dissolution of the number of the body, when death completes the number of the body. For the number is the union of the body. Now the body dies when it is not able to support the man. And this is death: the dissolution of the body and the destruction of the sensation of the body. And it is not necessary to be afraid of this, not because of this, but because of what is not known and is disbelieved one is afraid.

Likewise, in the Hindu scripture Katha Upanishad (sometimes known as "Death as Teacher"), we find the story of a young man, Nachiketa, who desires to know about life and death. He visits the abode of Yama, the King of Death, who offers him three boons. After the first two are satisfied (that Nachiketa's father will love him always, even upon his death, and instructions on performing the fire sacrifice), Nachiketa requests as the third boon to know what happens when a person dies.

"Some say the person still exists; others say he does not. I want you to teach me the truth," says Nachiketa.

Yama is reluctant. "It is very hard to know," he says, and tells Nachiketa to ask for something else—anything! Ask for "sons and grandsons who will live for a hundred years. Ask for herds of cattle, elephants and horses, gold and vast land; ask to live as long as you desire," says Yama. "Ask for beautiful women of loveliness rarely seen on earth, riding in chariots, skilled in music to attend you, Nachiketa. Don't ask me about the secret of death."

Finally, Yama relents, and for the rest of this scripture explains how Nachiketa can achieve happiness and peace in this life and how to be freed from the fear of death and attain liberation from rounds of birth and death by realizing the One, the Absolute Self or Brahman, by transcending ego and becoming one with this Absolute.

Grasping at and clinging to life does not bring us joy; it increases our fear of loss and death. We live less meaningfully when we seek to hold all as permanent and resist change—a natural part of life.

We cannot know death until we experience it. At that point, if we have not gotten beyond what is not known about death, it is too late. It happens anyway. It is not death that we should fear; what we should fear is our *fear of death,* for death is simply change. That is all death is—change from a manifested physical state to an unmanifest or nonphysical state. It is simply a change of our state of being in the physical body to a purely spiritual state. This is what some call the *soul* or what I have come to know as the *mind*, which resides in the heart chakra and endures throughout all lifetimes. This is what I believe survives death of the physical body.

Most people believe in some type of life after death, whether that is rebirth or reincarnation (as in Hinduism and Buddhism), in which we are reborn into a new body as an incarnate entity, or resurrection (Christianity), in which the old body is raised anew. Most people in Western culture believe there *must* be something of ourselves that survives the loss of the physical body—some form of our identity or self through which our life is lived and through which we attain meaning.

It can be difficult for Christians to understand what survives death. As a Christian growing up, I was never taught about this subject. "Your soul survives death" is what I'd most often hear, but no one could define the meaning of *soul*. What constitutes the soul? How do we die? What happens in the dying process? Where does the soul go? How does it get out of our body? It was all a great mystery, and that mystery makes death and dying process extremely fearsome.

One Buddhist teacher has observed that we are all one medical diagnosis away from having our lives change dramatically. Yet change is something most of us try to avoid. Human beings don't like change. Nevertheless, as Mark Cuban, the billionaire owner of the Dallas Mavericks, has written, "Where there is change there is opportunity." That is not how most of us look at it.

Typically, we see only disruption, being forced from the known in our lives into the unknown. We like our self-created ruts.

But change, like taxes and death, is unavoidable. It happens whether we like it (or plan for it) or not. Every day, our bodies change while we're going about the business of living. Old cells die and dissolve, and new cells appear without our having to think about it. We're not even close to being the same people we were yesterday, much less twenty years ago. Yet we hardly notice the small changes that are taking place in our lives every minute. Rather we think of change as big and sudden—those major, life-altering events that smack us between the eyes so that things are never quite the same. We make plans, and ZAP!—we get stopped in our tracks and detoured. (Detours can be good things, as I'll discuss. It's all in how we look at them.)

I've studied and practiced with these realities of change for more than two decades, but although it helps to study and practice, one is never fully prepared for change. During the summer of 2000, I had a premonition that something was about to happen with my best friend that would radically alter our friendship. I didn't know exactly what, but I began preparing for a change. It helps to be attentive to one's inner voice, as it often gives us hints of what is to come.

That September came a series of events—arson on their farm. A disgruntled worker set their barn on fire, burning many horses to death while others escaped into the surrounding desert, hurting themselves. My friend, her daughter, and her son-in-law were in Italy at the time, attending international equestrian events. On hearing the news, they flew home to pick up the pieces. Things would never be the same again. Their lives had changed drastically.

I grieved the loss of my friend's daughter's horses. I grieved the loss of their barn and a life that had seemed secure and idyllic. And when my friend announced not long after that tragedy that she would be moving to Canada (where her son-in-law was a citizen) to reestablish their lives on a farm northeast of Toronto, I grieved for myself. Change is difficult.

As I worked with that change, allowing myself to grieve the fact that my best friend would no longer be close by, and that our trips, our hikes in the mountain preserve, and other fun times would no longer be, I began to understand the Buddhist teaching that change always *is*. We cannot stop change from happening or make things different than they are. Working with change, embracing it, and acknowledging it as a fact of life is difficult but necessary if we are to learn to be happy in the face of change.

Life is unpredictable. That is its biggest challenge. Sometimes circumstances and situations move quickly. We walk out the door in the morning, and by evening our world has been turned upside down by an accident, a diagnosis of an acute illness, or a lover who has left us. Myriad things remind us that we do not control our lives. We are at the mercy of our human existence and the fragility of our physical bodies.

A colleague recently posted on Facebook that his wife of just three years died in her sleep at age fifty-seven. He awoke to find her lying beside him silent, still, and without life. It was so sudden and so unexpected! He is heartbroken and of course questioning why. Why her? Why now? She was so young! No one should die just when life seemed so perfect! But life can change so quickly and so unexpectedly that we are often left searching for answers.

THE JOURNEY

One of the big lessons I learned from Brent, my significant other of ten years, as I walked a journey of cancer and death with him, was nonattachment to outcomes. He believed that life is what it is, and that wanting it to be otherwise is at best an effort in futility. People who are diagnosed with terrible diseases chase cures, spending all their time on the Internet tracking down doctors, hospitals, and alternative therapies in an attempt to change the outcome. Brent did not choose that path. He believed in nonattachment to outcomes and did not want to spend the time he had left in this dimension trying to alter an outcome that he knew was probably inevitable: death. Rather, he embraced it.

I also learned that crisis produces an opportunity to stretch oneself spiritually, to grow, to realize what is important in life and what is not, and to become a more compassionate, caring, loving individual. If we see all events as opportunities to grow—even the events we do not want—we begin to understand their meaning to us. According to the great mythologist Joseph Campbell, there is no inherent meaning to life; we bring meaning to life through our experiences. Brent's illness became a test for me to see if the Buddhist practices I'd been engaged in over the previous ten years were really as beneficial for facing life's challenges as I'd been told they would be. I began to explore my previously held Christian beliefs, overlaying them with the Buddhist teachings that I had come to love. What about the God of my Christian upbringing? People who believe in God often blame him for their trials and sufferings. But who is this God?

That big conundrum—do we exist because of God, or does God exist because of us?—makes us stop and think about life, about why we are here and what comes after. For many people, suffering means there cannot be a God. For many others, God *is* suffering. For still others, God does not exist outside ourselves: we are not only the image of God, but we *are* God, a mirror image of our divine creator.

Brent had no fixed ideas about God or about religion except that he knew that religion, in the sense that he understood it, wasn't for him. He had given it up after he left for college. When his father died, Brent was only sixteen years old. He'd watched his father suffer for two years through surgeries and round after round of radiation and chemo treatments. It was 1959, and not much was known about cancer. All Brent knew was that his father suffered terribly trying to find the cure. When the end came, Brent was at peace with the whole event. He took one day off school for the funeral, then returned to his life.

Always the forward-looking person, always the one whose glass was half-full, always the optimist who believed in living in the now and not squandering time on "pity parties" or having anniversaries for events and people that were long past and gone, Brent somehow knew the secret of living a happy, fearless life. His mantra was, go with the flow. Never want things to be different than the way they are. Keep moving forward. Never look back. Be content with whatever life hands you and learn from every experience.

No, Brent was not a practicing Buddhist. He'd never even heard much about Buddhism until he met me in June 1994. He said that everything he believed and practiced came from an inner knowing that had been his guide since he was a boy of ten, in the hospital for the first time for eye surgery. As he lay in the hospital bed that night, awaiting surgery in the morning, he thought to himself, "I can either cry for my parents to be here, fight this whole surgery thing, and get upset that I have a bad eye, or I can just go somewhere else in my mind and accept that this is just the way it is."

Brent went somewhere else in his mind, and thus began his first experiment with mind over matter. It helped him in athletics as a semiprofessional hockey player. It helped him when his father died. It helped him through the many ups and downs of life, which included two divorces, career moves, jobs won and lost. It gave him the strength to become the person he was meant to be, and to be a happy, laidback guy with a great sense of humor about life—and, as we would discover, about death as well.

That was brought home to me swiftly one afternoon when, after an endoscopy procedure to determine why Brent was having such a difficult time swallowing, a doctor came to me in the waiting room and pronounced that it appeared to be esophageal cancer. The rest of his words became a blur. I thought my heart was going to stop right then and there. Fear gripped me like a vise.

When it comes to change, fear is a huge enemy. It makes us into monsters we didn't know existed inside us. We become angry, raging against this change as well as against the overwhelming thought of death. I read once that all fear is rooted in the fear of loss—of material goods, jobs, and especially of life. Fear of death is probably the one fear all sentient beings have in common, from the tiniest ant to the largest elephant. Although smaller beings with less expanded minds cannot label it fear, they know it instinctively and express it through methods of self-preservation. Put your finger down in front of an ant on the sidewalk and watch it run from you. That is instinctual fear.

Fear is rooted in a fear of loss: loss of possessions, loss of loved ones, and the biggest fear of all: loss of life. For most of us, overcoming fear is a lifelong effort. I've worked with my fears for many years, practicing various meditations to allay my fears of all the things that could happen to me, projecting unknown future events onto myself in the present.

Life at any point along the continuum is the result of our past choices. According to Eastern philosophies, it results from the karma (actions) these choices have created, or from the karma that was *not* created. The road is constantly branching out before us: quantum probabilities in the universe. We are free to make choices, which we call free will, knowing that each choice will have a different consequence or karmic result.

We tend to make choices based on our senses, our material wants and desires, all of which come from the ego, the little *self*, rather than making choices based on the higher *Self* or Higher Mind that is rooted in the Universal Mind. Fear is the obstacle to making the choices that move us beyond the self to the Self. Fear rules our lives every day until we learn that it is our worst enemy and we learn to live from faith.

What are we afraid of? Mostly of dying. Far too many of us spend our time and energy trying not to die, focusing on being safe and preventing any type of injury or possibility of death rather than trying to live better lives.

Most of our fear of death comes from misunderstanding reality. Strong identification with all that we believe to be real—especially the body—keeps us in constant fear of death. "We are consciously or unconsciously in a constant state of anxiety, because decay and death is what inevitably lies ahead for this walking-talking skin-bag," write Timothy Freke and Peter Gandy in *The Laughing Jesus: Religious Lies and Gnostic Wisdom*. They quote the ancient Stoic Epictetus, who taught, "It is your fear of death that terrifies you. You can think about a thing in many ways. Scrutinize your idea of death. Is it true? Is it helpful? Don't fear death. Rather, fear your fear of death."

Dying is easy. It's living that is difficult. I learned that lesson when Brent was diagnosed with esophageal cancer and given less than a year to live, even if he chose surgery, chemotherapy, and radiation. He chose only surgery and lived a good life for another eighteen months. He called it his "adventure," and because he lived so well—with nonattachment to outcomes, a go-with-the-flow attitude, and no fear—dying for him was very easy, something he expressed to me the day before he died. "Dying is so easy," he said softly. "I thought it would be harder than this, but it's so easy!" I replied that it was easy for him because he wasn't afraid to die.

I once heard a professional caregiver speak to a group of other caregivers. She said that in her eight years as a live-in caregiver for the terminally ill, she noticed recurring themes. Often people came to the end of their lives with one big regret: not being true to themselves. They had lived a life that others expected of them, but not the one they may have truly desired or would have been most fulfilling to them.

Fear of dying often creates difficult circumstances, not only for the person who is dying, but for the person's loved ones as well—parents, spouse, significant other, or best friend. They suffer fear of the unknown, not understanding mind, soul, consciousness, and life in terms of either scientific or Eastern philosophical concepts. Loved ones also fear their lives without the ones they love.

One must learn to die well even as one must learn to live well; the two are very much connected. In an article for *Parabola* magazine, Benedictine monk Brother David Steindl-Rast wrote that at the monastery, the monks are "counseled (or challenged) to have death at all times before our eyes." I also encountered that teaching as a Buddhist practitioner, with the admonition that death is certain; only the time of our death is uncertain. Being mindful of death every day is one way we learn to die well—and live well too.

My wish is that everyone would have a good death, as Brent did: dying quietly, peacefully, without fear, and free from attachments either to the body or to others. That will take an understanding of life, death, consciousness, and reality from each of us, especially doctors and other healthcare providers, who are often present in the face of death. As long as medical personnel are not comfortable with the dying process and unable to let go of the fact that some will die in their care, it will be difficult to reach a state of dying well, which also means living well.

Part 1

WHAT IS

LIFE?

1

WHY WE DON'T KNOW HOW TO DIE

F or the meaning of death and the meaning of life are inextricably linked. Death gives life meaning and life gives death its significance. Thus, we cannot truly know who we are or life's meaning or purpose until or unless we unravel the mystery of death. To understand life, first we must understand death and what it means to die.

—JOHN R. AUDETTE

We do not know how to die because we do not know how to live. We live in fear, greed, power, and desire for material things, including the desire to retain our physical bodies indefinitely. Researchers in laboratories are continually working on ways to make it possible to live far beyond the one-hundred-year lifespan that many are reaching today. They are attempting to do this by reducing stress on our cells so that they will not age. This is based on the belief that only an extremely long life is worth living and that putting death several hundred years into the future is the path to happiness.

Western culture contributes to our fears by restricting the pure enjoyment of being free to pursue the exciting and adventuresome activities that make us feel alive. Government rules and regulations constrict us to the narrow channel of "safety" until we are trapped in the illusion that by being "safe"—putting on our seat belts while riding through life—we will somehow escape the ultimate tragedy of death. Yet the ultimate tragedy of life is being prevented from really living life to the fullest. We pursue pleasure and eschew pain. We have become blinded by our senses and have forgotten our true home.

The beautiful Gnostic poem *The Hymn of the Pearl* tells the story of a young man who was sent from his home on a journey into a strange land. His parents, the king and queen of his homeland, gave him a bundle of precious jewels, removed his "robe of glory" and his purple toga, and then they wrote it in his heart so he would not forget:

> "When you go down into Egypt
> and bring back the One Pearl
> which lies in the middle of the sea
> and is guarded by the snorting serpent,
> you will again put on your robe of glory
> and your toga over it,
> and with your brother, our next in rank,
> you will be heir in our kingdom."

The young man did as he was told. He traveled the long distance to Egypt, went to the place where the serpent guarded the pearl, and settled into an inn while he waited for the serpent to fall asleep. The young man decided to disguise himself as one of the locals, so he put on a robe like those of the Egyptians:

> But somehow they learned
> I was not their countryman,
> and they dealt with me cunningly
> and gave me their food to eat.
> I forgot I was the son of kings,
> and served their king.
> I forgot the pearl
> for which my parents had sent me.
> Through the heaviness of their food
> I fell into a deep sleep.

When we journey into this level of consciousness that we call physical reality, our mind (or soul; the Greek word for *mind* is *psyche*, often translated as *soul*) "falls" into what we perceive to be a physical body of solid matter. At that point we become slaves of illusion, or *maya*, as the Eastern philosophies call it. Our gross-level mind creates the physicality that we experience, according to Buddhists as well as many of today's quantum physicists.

Our mind creates our own reality (which is why reality is different for every individual). Although we call it *reality*, it is an illusion. In the illusion of this perceived reality, we begin to partake of all that we see. We put on these clothes we call our physical bodies; we eat the food and partake of the enjoyments of this material world. We become heavy with the material possessions that own us as we grasp after them. We mistake the illusion for reality; as Plato explained many centuries ago, we mistake the shadows on the cave wall for the real thing. We have become materialists. We have fallen asleep.

Most of us in this world of *samsara*—the Sanskrit word for this world of illusion, delusion, and deception—are asleep. We fall victim to maya: a word used to describe tricks magicians perform in their shows. What we believe we are seeing and what is actually happening are two different things. This illusion is real, but it is not real in the way we believe it is. The white tiger that was on stage before our eyes suddenly disappears under a satin cloth and in a split second appears on a large shelf high above the audience. Or the elephant standing before us not twenty feet away vanishes in the blink of an eye, and the silk covering that hid the huge animal falls to the stage floor. This is illusion. All around us is reality to our five senses, but it is not real in the way we believe it is.

We are not fully awake and aware. We do not remember our past lives, where we came from, why we are here, or what being here actually means. We also fail to understand how we can attain happiness in this human life for ourselves and others. The young prince in *The Hymn of the Pearl* fell into this samsaric world—this physical world of illusion—and fell asleep. Overcome by the delusions of this world of maya, he forgot from whence he came or even why he'd been sent there.

The young man was not left to his own devices for long. He soon received a letter from his parents, the king and queen, reminding him of his duty, saying:

"Awake and arise from your sleep
and hear the words of our letter!
Remember that you are a son of Kings
and see the slavery of your life."

The one thing we must do on this level of consciousness is wake up. It becomes easy to forget who we are or why we are here because we are distracted by the phenomena of materiality, which our senses tell us are real, permanent, and important. Waking up means becoming fully conscious of who we really are and how reality exists and recognizing the impermanence of the world of matter, which has been created in the mind by the mind, as I have heard so many times from Buddhist teachers. We are not our bodies. We are not our social status or our jobs. We are not our bank accounts or our 401(k) plans.

There are times, however, when we are subtly reminded that there is something greater than this illusory world of materiality and that there is something we have to do other than accumulate the things of this world. Do we have a greater purpose? Why are we here? The king and queen remind the prince of this:

First, the letter instructed:
"Remember the pearl
for which you went into Egypt!"

How easy it is to get sidetracked! An editor once told me about the time he sent one of his senior writers to a convention in Las

Vegas. This writer had never been there before, and when he got into town, he was bedazzled by the neon lights, the glitz, the glamour and glitter of the Strip, and the gambling. He was so taken in by all this that he ignored the convention and played for three days. He didn't get one word of convention material for the magazine.

That's the way it is on this level of consciousness—in samsara. We become distracted and deluded by what we believe to be reality. We no longer remember our purpose.

Then the prince's parents tell him:

> "Remember your robe of glory
> and your splendid mantle
> which you may wear
> when your name is named in the Book of Life,
> is read in the book of heroes,
> when you and your brother inherit
> our kingdom."

Remember your true home and the things that really matter! Remember your heritage—that we are the children of the heavens, children of the universe! We have much to inherit that is everlasting and worthy of our divine natures. We shouldn't squander our lifetimes on things of illusion.

Yet it takes most of us the better part of our lives to learn what is really important. Maybe we'll wake up when we're forty or fifty years old! That is about the time when one begins to ask the big question that was made into Peggy Lee's popular song: "Is that all there is?" We've gone to school (the student years);

gotten married, established a career, bought a house, and had children (the householder years); and now, during this third stage of life, we are all settled, and life is perfect. Yet we ask ourselves, "Is that all there is?" The Hindu traditions tell us that this is time to prepare for the final stage in one's life—spiritual fulfillment, as we move towards the exit.

Life and death are closely entwined—two sides of the same coin. Brother David Steindl-Rast observes, "Birth and death come very close to one another: neither of the two events can be precisely pinned down to a moment in time."

We spend a lot of time preparing for our life, but what is life? "I can imagine that the very moment in which someone comes to life is also the moment in which he really dies," says Steindl-Rast. We are taught that living the best of life requires that we "die" to the world. So perhaps there are many small "deaths" along the way as we traverse this physical world seeking meaning and purpose.

We essentially don't know how to live well because we do not know how to die to the world of physical experience, to the distractions of the senses that lure us away from the life of the spirit. Like the young prince who was sent from his true home to experience life on another level of consciousness and was led astray by the illusion of it all, we too lose our way in the morass of illusion that *this*—life on the physical plane—is all there is. We partake of the material things that life in this world offers us and are caught up in the illusion that what we apprehend with our senses is real and permanent. We become attached to all that we see, feel, hear, taste, and smell. We believe that there is inherent, solid reality in all that we experience in this realm;

as a result, the experiences become the reality. That makes dying—leaving this plane of existence, and all that we've accumulated materially, for something that is unknown—extremely difficult.

In *The Power of Now*, Eckhart Tolle notes that "we live in a culture that is almost totally ignorant of death, as it is almost totally ignorant of anything that truly matters." We spend a lot of time thinking about our goals and desires in life and what we want out of it, but we rarely ponder death. Rarely do we seek to gain a full understanding of the impermanence of material possessions and especially of our bodies. We do not understand the mind and the role consciousness plays in creating the material world. Because we do not understand how we create the world and our lives, we do not understand what death is or how we die, which results in our fear of death.

The twentieth-century spiritual teacher Jiddu Krishnamurti wrote that living has to be more than just clinging to life because one is afraid to die. "If one does not know what living is one cannot know what death is—they go together. If one can find out what the full meaning of living is, the totality of living, the wholeness of living, then one is capable of understanding the wholeness of death. But one usually enquires into the meaning of death without enquiring into the meaning of life." Conversely, we spend a lot of time seeking the meaning and purpose of life without exploring death and the meaning of death.

As human beings in the physical body, we identify with our body to such a degree that the thought of leaving it becomes almost unbearable. Who am I without my body? Do I still exist? What is the future of life, including this unknown territory of death?

CHOOSING THE PATH

After being diagnosed with cancer, Brent was instructed to see an oncologist for the next steps. He went to the oncologist with CT films in hand. The doctor looked at the scans and shook his head. "This is very serious stuff," he said, frowning. "You can die soon, so we need to start chemotherapy immediately, followed by radiation, then surgery, then more chemotherapy."

"I know I will die soon," replied Brent, with an amazingly positive attitude. Because of this, the doctor may have thought he was taking the situation too lightly. Few could understand Brent's almost total fearlessness in dealing with his situation. Since his experience with his father's death and his determination not to fear anything in life, he'd achieved a level of courage that few people have. Life for him was an adventure—all of it.

"I'm not afraid to die," Brent told the oncologist matter-of-factly. It wasn't the right thing to say to someone whose primary business is selling chemotherapy to people desperate to live. The oncologist was taken aback.

The idea behind that treatment regimen was to destroy all the cancer with chemo and radiation, then do surgery, after which Brent would receive yet another round of chemo and hope the cancer would not return and spread.

Brent told the oncologist that he was not going to have chemo or radiation because his father had died a horrible death from stomach cancer while undergoing these treatments. The oncologist became very irate, telling Brent, "Don't you know you'll die if you don't have chemotherapy?"

"Dude, I'm going to die anyway, but I want to live the best life I can live until then," Brent insisted. "I'm not doing chemo."

"Well, then, there's nothing I can do for you," the doctor replied tersely and stomped out of the room, slamming the door behind him.

"This is just another part of the adventure," Brent said later that evening. The oncologist had said that even if Brent had every treatment available—radiation, chemo, and surgery—he had only a 20 to 30 percent chance of living longer than a year. Not the greatest odds. Nothing we'd ever bet on, for sure!

* * *

We do not know the future. We *should not* know the future. Our past is folded into the present, and our future is unfolding in our present, so that what we did yesterday creates our today, and what we do today creates our tomorrow—only it's always today! We have no future in the true sense of the word. According to quantum physicists, and Eckhart Tolle, the future truly is now.

The past creates unhappiness for us because we blame it for our present feelings. Past wrongs and past experiences often linger to torture us today because we have not learned to let go of the past. The future creates all kinds of problems for us as well because of our misguided anticipations, fears, and expectations of what will be. The road to hell is paved with unmet expectations! We suffer long before anything actually happens, and we suffer even more when our anticipation of the future turns out to be not what we expected.

There is a Buddhist dharma lesson that says:

> Do not pursue the past;
> Do not lose yourself in the future.
> The past no longer is,
> the future has not yet come.
> Looking deeply at life as it is in the very here and now
> the practitioner lives in stability and freedom.

I am sure that during my life on the astral plane (or wherever this entity that would become me was prior to this lifetime), I made a sacred contract with my spirit guide, agreeing to do exactly what I was called to do. We hear people say there are no accidents, but this is not to say that there is no free will. Certainly, free will plays a part in our lives in that we are always free to choose a path that is put before us. There are also no accidents, in the sense that every circumstance, every situation, every person we meet along the path helps give our life meaning and purpose. Each choice we make over a lifetime of living gives our lives purpose and meaning. All of life is for a purpose, not some purpose out there somewhere, but the purpose that is unfolding within each of us each moment of each day. Every event brings meaning to our lives. As Joseph Campbell observed when asked about the meaning of life in a Bill Moyers interview, "There is no meaning to life; we bring meaning to it."

Living in our physical bodies is about uncovering our purpose. It gives us a means of experiencing a different dimension of consciousness, a place away from our "home," and one that challenges our ability to recognize illusion versus reality. The experiences that we have in these physical bodies give us purpose and lead us, as seekers, back home.

Life in this three-dimensional world is about change and impermanence, neither of which we humans like to acknowledge or accept. It is about pain and suffering and death. That is what Prince Siddhartha, who would become the Buddha, set out to uncover, searching to discover why we suffer and die. The Four Noble Truths that the Buddha received at his enlightenment are so called because they are truths for all of us experiencing this physical, material universe.

The First Noble Truth is that life in this realm is pain and suffering. Everyone suffers. Each person may experience a different kind of suffering or experience suffering differently, but we all suffer, nonetheless. I have a friend whose ex-sister-in-law has a horrible mental disorder, which causes her to wreak havoc in her own life and in the lives of her children and ex-husband. When she is on medication, she understands just how painful she has made life for people that she loves and how painful her own life is. That is the way life is for most of us, even those of us who do not have mental disorders as such. (In a way, we all have a disorder in that we see the material world that our mind creates as reality. We are deluded into believing that this is all there is.)

There is, however, a way to transcend pain and suffering. It calls for embracing the very thing that causes us these discomforts, accepting it as part of our path, and moving or flowing with it. The Second Noble Truth is key: suffering occurs only when we want things in our lives to be different than they are, only when we fight against the situation. When we can't accept and embrace the opportunities presented by change, and when we can't even see that change can be an opportunity for something wonderful to happen, we experience suffering. When we want things to be different and believe that there is no purpose or reason to events, rather than seeing opportunity, we see punishment. We begin to cry, "Why me?"

Who hasn't at one time or another wanted life to be different than it is? It's human to believe our thoughts about ourselves and our lives, to buy into the illusion that life should be different than it is, that if we have the right job, marry the right spouse, and have all the right toys, we will live happily ever after. We spend a lot of time in "if only" land. "If only" I had a different job; "if only" I had a larger house, a newer car, more money, different parents, a better upbringing.

Buddhist teachers tell us that we can use all situations in our lives as means to enlightenment, even those we do not like or want. In fact, those challenging situations bring to us the best opportunities for spiritual growth.

In his book *No Man Is an Island*, Thomas Merton tells us that the "mystery of death, more terrible and sometimes more cruel than ever, remains incomprehensible to men who, though they know they must die, retain a grim and total attachment to individual life as if they could be physically indestructible." In the Buddhist way, we contemplate our own death on a daily basis. We take this time to practice the art of dying—the process of letting go of our physical bodies before we are confronted with immediacy of our death.

Attachment, particularly to our bodies and the enjoyments of this world (we rarely remember all the trials and tribulations of life as we lay dying) is truly the root of suffering, as the Buddha taught. We are attached to "I" and "myself" and "me" and "my life" as if these things were inherently real and permanent. We all know in our deepest heart of hearts that our bodies are impermanent, and death is the way of all the earth, yet we live as if that were not true.

Not knowing when or how we will die perhaps causes us the greatest fear. Freud said that the "dread of death" is the basis for our failure to live "authentically in the world with no fear of death to prevent our living life to the utmost."

The Indian guru Sri Aurobindo says, "Death has no reality except as a process of life," which is something we fail to understand. Life and death are not separate but are part of the same process. "Even in the death of the body there is no cessation of Life . . . . All renews itself, nothing perishes," says Aurobindo. This renewal is not generally understood. Some traditions call it *rebirth* or *reincarnation*; the Christian tradition calls it *resurrection*. Almost all religious and spiritual traditions believe in the continuance of this thing we call "life," but very few help people understand what lives, what merely transitions to another level of consciousness, and what dies. "All existence here is a universal Life that takes the form of Matter," Aurobindo explains.

It is becoming attached to the "form," or our bodies, and the things of this world that causes us pain and suffering when we think of death. Allowing ourselves to achieve a state of nonattachment is ideal for approaching the death of the body. "If one clings to the idea of 'me,' that 'me' which one believes must continue, the 'me' that is put together by thought, including the 'me' in which one believes there is the higher consciousness, the supreme consciousness, then one will not understand what death is in life," writes Krishnamurti. And which of us does *not* cling to the idea of an inherently existent "I"?

The Mother, who taught with Sri Aurobindo at his ashram in Pondicherry, India, tells us that death is not what we believe it to be. Since those of us in the West were primarily reared in a Judeo-Christian tradition, we are often bewildered by the Eastern idea of death, particularly rebirth or reincarnation. The Mother notes that we expect death to be this "natural quietness of an unconscious rest" but then tells us that it will be that only if we "prepare for it." The mind—the mental continuum, as it is called in Buddhist philosophy—is a storehouse of all the experiences of body, speech, and mind that we have stored up throughout our many lifetimes, and those experiences don't just disappear when we die. We carry our thoughts, speech, attitudes, hatreds, and loves with us into the next realm. "All that belongs to the vital world does not disappear with the material substance, all your desires, attachments, cravings persist with the sense of frustration and disappointment, and all that prevents you from finding the expected peace," the Mother writes. "To enjoy a peaceful and eventless death you must prepare for it. And the only effective preparation is the abolition of desires."

Desirelessness is a practice that helps us move beyond our attachments to life as we want it to be. Nevertheless, we all want life to be exactly the way we want it—patted down, buttoned up, safe and secure. The popularity of books such as *The*

Secret, which has sold millions of copies worldwide, shows how desperately people want to direct their lives and have what they believe they want or will make them happy. Thus, they want to know the "secret" to attracting to themselves the life they want.

There is a real problem with wanting in this way: we do not actually *know* what will make us happy or teach us the lessons we need to learn. We always think we know what we want, so our desires become mired in the things of this level of consciousness. The "secret" of intention actually works. The problem is, once we get what we think we want, we might find out that our lives are more miserable than before.

Another cause for pain and suffering is our attachment to outcomes. We want life to work out as we have it imagined in our minds; we've written the script for our projected future. I've found myself in that mode, saying, "It wasn't supposed to be this way!"

Oh, really? Well, just how *was* it supposed to be? Attachment to outcomes often leads us to miss the lessons we need to learn. Maybe life doesn't turn out the way we wanted it to, or the way we expected or imagined. But ultimately life happens in the way that is necessary for us, within the play of karma, to learn lessons and grow spiritually.

On my path, I learned that out of crisis comes opportunity—opportunity to stretch oneself spiritually, to grow, to realize what is and what is not important in life and become a more compassionate, caring, loving individual. If we see all events, even those we do not want, as opportunities to grow, we begin to understand their meaning in our life, which also brings more purpose to our life. Our life events are not random or chaotic or accidental but are purposeful and full of meaning for us if we look deep enough to realize it. As many philosophers teach us, there is no *inherent* meaning to life. We bring meaning to life through our experiences.

People reared in the Judeo-Christian tradition often thank God for their blessings and curse God for their hardships. They say, "Why did God do this to me?" Why indeed? Who, in fact, created our life? Who carries the karma for life events to unfold as they do? Who makes the choices that result in both good and bad consequences (if we want to judge them that way), and who chooses to see life as a duality of good and bad? Perhaps *all is good*! We just need a different perspective.

2

WHY WE DON'T UNDERSTAND LIVING AND DYING

Jean-Yves Leloup, author of *The Gospel of Mary Magdalene*, a commentary on a lost Gnostic gospel rediscovered in 1986, notes that it teaches us about karma. Karma is typically thought of as a concept in Eastern philosophy, but it is actually a universal law of cause and effect that is evident in all times and places. Like gravity, karma is always present and is always acting upon us, whether we like it or not. The concept appears in the Old and New Testaments, the Kabbalah, the Qur'an, the Bhagavad Gita, and in many other texts.

This doctrine teaches that there is no one to blame for sickness, pain, or the circumstances in life; rather, everything is the result of our karma. We are responsible for our lives, our attitudes, our beliefs about ourselves, and our place in samsara. Leloup writes, "Even death—or what you might imagine to be death—is the consequence of your actions and attitudes. That which you call death is the expression of a disordered intellect that has long ago identified your *self* with your mortal body, along with its thoughts, emotions, and mortal attachments. . . . This disordered perception is the fruit of your corrupted nature."

One morning, at the age of five, my grandson tearfully announced to his mother that he was sad because he could no longer remember what God looks like. Like my grandson, we've lost the memory of our divine nature. Consequently, we become attached to what we think we know: this world and all its supposed realities and its many illusions. Attachment is the root of suffering, because attachment is born of the desire to possess things, especially life. We read about many people who demand that the doctors do all they possibly can to save them or a loved one. Pull out all the stops! Spend all the money possible to save a life at all costs, no matter the suffering involved. But attachment is not compassion. Attachment is selfishness born of ego.

Embrace life. Embrace death. Learn how to live well, and you will know how to die well. That's the key to happiness in the Buddhist sense. Indeed, it is the key to happiness no matter what spiritual philosophy one practices. Embrace whatever we encounter in life. Learn the lessons we need to carry through to our subsequent lives.

It helps to believe in karma, because it solves the age-old question of why bad things happen to good people. The Bible says, "As ye sow, so also shall ye reap." There is a reason: karma. It is the ultimate form of justice.

If we believe in a just God, we must believe in karma. Often people believe that an unjust God has allowed their loved one to die or be killed in a traffic accident. Accidents don't make sense, but karma helps us understand that it isn't God beating up on us: whatever the circumstances, at some point along the continuum of our lives, we performed the actions that created the karma. No one is to blame. Karma is one of the universal principles that hold true no matter who you are or what your belief system is.

The Old Testament story of Job shows karma at work. Job was afflicted with much suffering because of a bet that Satan made with Yahweh, the God of the Old Testament. Satan asked God if he could test and try Job in order to see what motivated him to love and obey God. Was it just that Job was a healthy, wealthy man who had all the material things of life? Or did Job truly love and obey God out of his heart?

After losing all his wealth and health, a downtrodden Job still worshipped God and believed that his life was worth it. Ultimately Job learned that his changing situation wasn't caused by God—or even Satan—but was just a consequence of his karma. As Elihu, one of Job's interlocutors, says, "Therefore harken unto me, ye men of understanding: far be it from God that he should do wickedness; and from the Almighty, that he should commit iniquity. For the work of a man shall he render unto him, and cause every man to find according to his ways, Yes, surely God will not do wickedly, neither will the Almighty pervert judgment" (Job 34:10–12).

It's all about karma. It's about having the life we ourselves created and need in order to progress spiritually and uncover the true nature of mind—our true inner and divine nature. Even God does not stand in the way of whatever we need to experience in this life to progress spiritually.

Neither does God cause our suffering. Someone once said that God is not the maker of the movie, only the projectionist. When people ask, "Why did God do this to me?" the answer is, "He didn't. This is your karma, either from some action in this life or in a previous life that ripened at this moment. It is the perfect time and place for this to ripen in your life; the perfect teacher to provide you with what you need to learn in order to experience your divine nature."

Many people do not like the idea of karma or of accepting responsibility for their lives. They find it difficult to believe that suffering, especially self-created suffering, should be a part of life. But remember that suffering is a state of mind; it arises when we see events and situations as a punishment. Suffering is a perspective that is relative to every individual. Just as happiness and the causes of happiness are different in each person's life, suffering and the causes of suffering are also different.

In Buddhism even happiness is referred to as "changing suffering," because what makes us happy one day is often the cause of our suffering the next day. Most people would say that the day of their marriage was the happiest day of their life. Yet five years later, the marriage is in shambles, and they are getting divorced. Here, marriage was the cause of their suffering. As our situations, conditions, and perceptions of life change, so does our idea of happiness and suffering. As our desires change, we experience the seesaw of happiness and suffering. It is the way life is in samsara.

Overcoming fear is key to being happy and content in this life. Why? Because fear disables us spiritually and physically; it stands in the way of our faith. "Fear not," Jesus says.

He mentions fear many times in the New Testament Gospels and stresses the importance of fearlessness. Fear destroys faith. Faith is the essence of fearlessness. "Why are ye so fearful? How is it that ye have no faith?" Jesus asked his disciples when they were in a ship on the Sea of Galilee during a terrible storm.

Does that mean we are never fearful? No, we are all fearful. But we can learn to transcend our fears by seeing that they are based in illusion, much like those in Harry Potter's school, Hogwarts, when the students of wizardry were learning the "Ridikkulus!" spell. Each student was instructed to use thought power to conjure up the thing he or she was most afraid of. Once the thing feared—the monster or whatever—became a "reality," the student had to face it, point at it, and shout "Ridikkulus!" With that, the feared thing became what it really was—a small, insignificant thing that could easily be done away with. This story teaches us that our thoughts create our fears, which become our reality. We can learn to face, then embrace, our fears and transform them into the reality of our faith.

Yes, something will get us. You don't get out of this world alive! Something will eventually cause us to leave our physical bodies—if not disease or accident, then surely old age. Fear of everything that may cause us harm or death is engulfing Americans in neurosis. Everything can hurt us. Everything can cause us pain or result in our death. Yet if one believes, as many spiritual seekers do, that there are no accidents, only karmic paths, all the fearmongering is in vain. There will be so-called accidents, but these events can be viewed as the results of our choices or our karma. There will be disease and there will ultimately be death for every living being, from the smallest amoeba to the largest elephant, from kings and presidents to the rag pickers on the garbage heaps of developing countries. Always be prepared for death, and do not fear.

The Judeo-Christian worldview fosters the fear of death with its idea that time is linear and limited: we have a beginning and follow that along a linear timeline to the end. Beyond that lies some enigma that Christians call *heaven*, which, if we are good enough and lucky enough, we will inhabit for all eternity. Not much is known about this heaven except that getting there is a roll of the dice. (Einstein said, "God does not play dice," but I think there's a bit of that going on in this scenario.) Christians are promised heaven if they obey all the rules, but we never know what all the rules are. Being good is relative, and even if the Christian thinks they are good, are they good enough?

For the Christian, the idea of heaven and hell presents some real questions. I know that it did for me, especially the idea that only Christians could go to heaven, which would leave out a lot of others who are doomed to the punishments of hell. Many Christians live their lives doubting whether they can make it to heaven and fear what happens if they don't.

In his book *God Is Red: A Native View of Religion* Vine Deloria Jr., an American Indian professor and lawyer, remarks that the Christian idea of heaven and hell creates a fear of death that native peoples do not have. "Tribal peoples, who had no difficulty with death, and saw it as part of a natural progression in the stages of life, seem to have no memory of promises of specific delights and rewards. However, they have a healthy attitude toward death that is a result of living completely within the normal cycles of life and death."

Fear is the antithesis of faith. Fear will get you, even if nothing else does. Fear draws you to that which you fear. What you fear becomes your reality, even if it was not a reality to begin with. Fear of death pervades our Judeo-Christian society. It is costing our government billions of dollars in unnecessary medical tests and drugs in an effort to keep people alive at all costs—even those who are obviously nearing death. We do not have a general spiritual understanding of death, because we lack an understanding of life. And life always involves death, at every level of existence. How can we live a fearless life if we are constantly in fear of the specter of death? We can't. It's that simple.

Deloria believes that at least "some of this fear of death derives from the message of Christianity itself": the portrayal of theology as "unnatural to the creation and as an evil presence resulting from the disobedience of Adam in the Garden of Eden." Lending fear to the Christian theology of death, Deloria adds, is the idea of the day of judgment,

> when the good and evil deeds of people would be evaluated, the good going to heaven and the evil and unbaptized people going to hell or to some intermediate place where they can congregate until released.

> The Indian ability to deal with death was a result of the much larger context in which Indians understood life.

Human beings were an integral part of the natural world and in death they contributed their bodies to become the dust that nourished the plants and animals that had fed people during their lifetime. . . . Death simply became another transitional event in a much longer scheme of life.

Sri Aurobindo explains death by saying that "the Force" or the "Life-force," the élan vital, the dynamic energy that "maintains life in the body . . . has suspended its outer operations but still informs the organized substance" which we call the body. This organized substance "does not leave immediately—and can be reactivated" (such as in a near-death experience) until "the process of disintegration has begun. . . . Even then there is life in the body, but a Life that is busy only with the process of disintegrating the formed substance (the body) so that it may escape in its elements and constitute with them in new forms. The Will in the universal Force that held the form together, now withdraws from constitution and supports instead a process of dispersion. Not until then is there the real death of the body." Aurobindo tells us:

> Life is everywhere, secret or manifest, organized or elemental, involved or evolved, but universal, all-pervading, imperishable; only its forms differ. . . . Life reveals itself as essentially the same everywhere from the atom to man, the atom containing the subconscious stuff and movement of being which are released into consciousness in the animal, with plant life as a midway stage of in the evolution. Life

is really a universal operation of Conscious-Force acting subconsciously on and in Matter. . . . Mind (not the brain) is an energy force of intelligence, which translates to Life; transforms into matter and forms.

Failure to understand what life is, how life takes form in matter, and why death is a part of life is what makes such organizations as Death with Dignity (formerly the Hemlock Society), such pariahs. We have all heard of Terri Schiavo, the young woman who lay in a hospice in Florida for more than a decade because her heart had stopped. She was put into a vegetative state by doctors who were attempting to save her. Her family and her husband fought over whether she should be allowed to die or remain alive. Her husband said she wouldn't have wanted to live in that vegetative state, while her parents felt that she would awaken and come back to normal any minute. Finally, a court ordered her feeding tube removed, and she died a few weeks later. An autopsy proved that she had no consciousness at all: no sight, no hearing, nothing. Her physical brain had shrunk down to a third of its normal size, atrophying beyond any capability of recovery.

This fight to keep people alive at all costs is not one we should be having in this country, but we see death as a final and horrible fate. This despite the fact that Christians profess to believe that heaven is a wonderful place where we should all be happy to take up residence and live in bliss forever. Obviously, many Christians don't truly believe that. A bumper sticker I saw once said, "All Christians want to go to heaven: they just don't want to die to get there."

Aurobindo writes that the law of death involves change and the "principle of succession" through time as the soul "moves through successive fields, successive experiences or lives, successive accumulations of knowledge, capacity, enjoyment" that it holds in subconscious memory. "This then is the necessity and justification of Death, not as a denial of Life, but as a process of Life; death is necessary because eternal change of form is the sole immorality to which the finite living substance can aspire and eternal change of experience . . . can attain." The "phenomenon of death involves . . . a struggle to survive, since death is the only negative term in which Life hides from itself . . . to seek for immortality. Precisely because the struggle for survival, the impulse towards permanence is contradicted by the law of death, we seek permanence for ourselves." At some level, we believe that life as we know it in matter should be permanent, which makes death all the more fearsome.

In Hinduism and Buddhism, one does not have to die to experience *moksha* or nirvana—spiritual liberation. Nirvana, which is purely a state of mind, can be experienced in this life, in samsara, if one has learned to see things differently and realized how life and death are part of the grand scheme of the cycles of birth, death, and rebirth.

Cultures such as those in the Far East see death as a beautiful, experiential transition to the next realm, where one awaits one's next birth into yet another life. The transition is eased through a series of rituals, including the reading of texts such as *The Tibetan Book of the Dead*, to help the soul leave peacefully and gently. It is said that people who fight death have a difficult time on the astral plane or the *bardo* state, as Tibetan

Buddhists call it. An adept Buddhist monk, on the other hand, can will his soul to leave his body when he knows it is time. The Native Americans too had a ritual in which, when death was near, they would go off and die peacefully, willing the soul to leave the body. Death is an honorable end to a life well lived.

Death is something that we do alone, but to die well is not a passive activity. Death is not something that happens to us; we can participate in it once we know how to die. Sometimes this process can take days or weeks before the final breath is drawn, or death can come quickly with hardly a moment to think about it. Hence, we need to be prepared for our death. Brother David Steindl-Rast writes about two German Catholic theologians who "put much weight on their ideas of what happens in a person's last moments. I would much rather say: Die when you are alive, because you don't know how well you will be able to do something that takes all your energy when you are senile, weak or very sick."

3

LIVING WITH SUFFERING: HOW NOT TO SUFFER

When they read the first of his Four Noble Truths—life is suffering (*dukkha* in Sanskrit)—many people believe that the Buddha was very negative. They don't understand why he wouldn't have been more "positive" in his teachings.

As I pointed out in the previous chapter, suffering is a state of mind. It is the way we perceive an event or a situation that causes us to suffer. Diving deeper into this teaching, we learn that because of our perceptions, we are the creators of our own suffering.

The Buddha taught that there are three roots of suffering: attachment, aversion, and ignorance. Attachment is the first and arises from desire brought on by the senses. We smell something good to eat and we desire to eat it; we see a shiny new car in our favorite color and feel a sense of wanting a new car to rise up. We see a handsome or beautiful person and we desire to have that person.

One of our greatest attachments is to our bodies. We completely identify with our bodies, because they represent who we are: *I* am thin, or *I* am fat; *I* am beautiful, or *I* am ugly. We identify so much with our bodies that we spend many hours a week grooming ourselves to make ourselves look beautiful or handsome so that someone will desire us. Attachment to our bodies is a primary cause of our fear of death—our bodies are *US!* Without our bodies, we are nothing. Yet they are impermanent. Cells live for varying lengths of time, but they reproduce continually as they die off and are replaced with new cells. Individual cells have finite lifespans. For example, white blood cells live for about thirteen days; cells of the epidermis (the outer skin) live for about thirty days; red blood cells live for about 120 days; and liver cells live for about eighteen months. While our bodies experience these little "deaths," we don't even realize they're happening. There is no pain or suffering during these cell deaths.

Ultimately, we are really not the same person this year as we were last year. In spite of these changes, we are attached to our bodies, because we believe them to be a permanent part of who we are. In his book *Letting Go of the Person You Used to Be*, Lama Surya Das says that we do not choose pain, but we do choose suffering. Pain is a part of our physical condition, but suffering is something we create in our mind, and it is relative to the person who is doing the suffering. For a teenager who spends five hours a day on social media, suffering is losing their cell phone. For another, it is being unable to afford their favorite car. Some days I choose suffering when I choose to wallow in the past and allow memories of things no longer of any consequence to take over my mind. We can even become attached to suffering. Although it is a waste of energy, I know people who do this because it gets them attention or causes others to feel sorry for them. This in turn feeds their suffering, and it becomes a vicious cycle.

Why do we choose this *dukkha* when the alternative is to embrace all that we experience as the path? We find ourselves asking, "Why me?" I do not know the answer to that. Perhaps attachment—even to suffering—is a part of being human, a way to enlarge the ego. Whenever we choose suffering, it is usually the result of being unable to see the big picture from this limited vantage point and let go of the mind that is creating suffering.

Karma plays a role in suffering as well. In his book *Good Life, Good Death: Tibetan Wisdom on Reincarnation,* Buddhist monk Nawang Gehlek Rinpoche says that his father once told him, "Whenever any kind of suffering comes, even a tremendous amount of suffering, it is our karma. If we don't pay for our own karma, who will?" Pain is inherently a part of life in the physical body, but suffering arises from the mind when we have aversion to what comes along in life that we do not like.

Aversion is the second cause of suffering. A circumstance or situation comes up in our life that causes us mental, emotional, or physical pain. We immediately resist it, because it is not what we want, and it causes suffering. However, the resistance causes even more suffering. There is, as some believe, a Law of Attraction, the idea that our thoughts and feelings bring to us what we focus on. This law brings about attachment—what we are attracted to we typically become attached to as well. Because of the duality we experience on this plane of existence, the Law of Attraction sets the Law of Resistance in motion. When we are attracted to something, we also have an aversion to its opposite. When we set our minds on what we want we are also setting our minds on what we *don't* want, and that sets us up for suffering.

Shauna Shapiro, PhD, teacher, author, and professor of psychology at Santa Clara University specializing in mindfulness training, has an interesting formula: S = P x R: *suffering = pain x resistance*. If, for example, you have ten units of pain times ten units of resistance, you will have one hundred units of suffering. A saying in the Religious Science (Science of Mind) tradition is, "What you resist persists." The more we resist anything in life, the greater the suffering we will create for ourselves.

Lama Surya Das tells the story of a woman who approached the Buddha and desperately begged him to restore her dead child to life. The Buddha told her that he would do so if she would go and find a mustard seed from a home where no one had ever died. The woman searched for many years but could not find a home where no one had ever died. She then realized the lesson the Buddha was trying to teach her: everyone suffers loss; everyone dies.

The third root of suffering, as the Buddha taught, is ignorance in the sense that we do not know the truth of reality. We do not know how things truly exist. We go through life believing or expecting all things to be permanent and that this is reality. The trees in my front yard appear to be solid and to truly exist as trees. The entire environment around us has the appearance of a solid, permanent way of being that we call reality. We suffer when we one day discover that what we thought was solid, permanent reality is merely illusion, an appearance that we perceive to be real yet does not exist as we believe it does.

Several years ago, during the winter rainy season in California, there was a news story about a woman who was losing her home to torrential rains. They were causing her beautiful, sprawling backyard to slide piece by piece into the ocean below. She had lived on the Northern California coast for forty years and had gradually watched pieces of her land fall into the ocean, but she had never thought that the day would come when not only her backyard but her whole house would collapse. She watched her home of forty years gradually break apart and slide down the cliff—an event she had never imagined. As this woman discovered, even the ground beneath our feet is impermanent.

Living in opposition to our environment—in opposition to what *is*—causes us stress, enhances our fears, and causes us to suffer. We are connected to the entire universe and all beings in it. When we live in opposition to what is, we go off balance, which creates stress and illness. Some schools of thought hold that illness is the result of the body and spirit being out of balance with the natural flow of life. Living in opposition means fighting against the unwanted situations that come into our lives; it is wanting life to be different.

Christmas Humphreys, a student of Zen Buddhism during the early twentieth century and founder of the Buddhist Society in London, writes in his book *Western Approach to Zen* that when applying the principles of the teachings,

First, we must learn to accept what comes to us, completely, willingly. At present we resent what we do not like; we are annoyed at what causes suffering; project, as the psychologists say, on to everyone else the blame that lies in ourselves and, generally refuse to accept the consequences of folly. Yet it is right that we should suffer precisely as we do; the very universe should burst asunder if it were not so. In brief, we must begin to face the most difficult thought in the field of Buddhism, that "It's all right," all of it, entirely all of it. Thus, and thus only should we face each situation just as it is. If we merely wish that it were something different, how can we do what needs to be done and do it well? We must learn to withhold our perpetual like and dislike, our doubt as to whether it is what is ought to be. We must learn to say YES to everything, whatever it may be.

In the United States, fighting is a good thing. "She's a fighter" is what people say about a strong, willful person who lets nothing stand in her way of living life. It's a compliment. When people are terminally ill and approaching death yet continuing to take medical treatment and doing everything possible to stay alive, people say, "He's a fighter." You don't hear anyone say, "He embraced his disease." What's that? Someone who gives up and caves in? That's not the American way!

To embrace our situation, to turn all adverse conditions into the path, requires that we see all conditions and situations as beneficial to our spiritual growth. In the final chapter of

Through the Gates of Gold by Theosophist Mabel Collins, who wrote this work in 1885, I came across this passage in the chapter titled "The Secret of Strength":

> There is only one way of escape from this terrible danger [the things in life that assail us and would destroy us] which we battle against every hour. Turn round, and instead of standing against the forces, join them; become one with Nature, and go easily upon her path. Do not resist or resent the circumstances of life any more than the plants resent the rain and the wind. Then suddenly to your own amazement, you find you have time and strength to spare, to use in the great battle which it is inevitable every man must fight—that in himself, that which leads to his own conquest.

She then talks about how, when we begin to embrace the reality of life and accept the circumstances of our lives, we forget the individual self:

> When he is thus indifferent to its welfare, the individual self grows more stalwart and robust, like the prairie grasses and the trees of untrodden forests. It is a matter of indifference to him whether this is so or not. Only, if it is so, he has a fine instrument ready in his hand; and in due proportion to the completeness of his indifference to it is the strength and beauty of his personal self.

The words most often associated with cancer are *fight* and *battle*. Cancer is seen as the invader—some alien, outside force that enters us to destroy us, so we must fight this invader. How many times do we see an obituary that reads, "She died after a long battle with cancer" or, "He lost his two-year battle with cancer." In war, where there are battles, there are winners and losers. And we all know which one it is better to be.

No one wants to be a loser. In the present culture, death is the equivalent of losing. You die, you've lost. How terrible, right? Doctors are extremely reluctant to talk about death and dying with terminally ill patients. They fear death almost as much as their patients do and believe that if their patient dies, it somehow represents a failure on their part. Maybe we need to readjust our thinking in this regard. Perhaps if you die, you've won! Perhaps it is a victory over life. That would be a twist. Perhaps the losers are those of us who have to remain in these bodies on this three-dimensional earth and continue to struggle to find ourselves and the path. Perhaps those who die are the real winners!

Disease and death are *not* the enemy. Jesus pointed out that what destroys the body is not to be feared or fought, but only what destroys the soul. The body, while necessary for performing our duties as humans, isn't really all that important. Disease can destroy us only if we allow it to define our life, to control us and rob us of our ability to experience joy by transcending the pain. By embracing the disease, we give it its proper place in our lives.

Some say that by refusing to acknowledge the existence of disease, we do not allow it to control us. Yet that is not what love is about. It is about embracing the disease, being grateful for the lessons it can bring, and loving life despite the disease. To believe that disease and death are a natural part of the human experience is to enable ourselves to know God's love in a unique way, more so than by refusing, rejecting, and insisting that pain, disease, and death should not be a part of life.

Cancer, after all, isn't some alien invader. Cancer is composed of our own cells, our own DNA. That is why cancer researchers are finding that almost every individual responds differently to every treatment and that treatments must be customized to the individual's DNA. Cancer is a part of us; it's just a part of us that is out of control. Perhaps embracing the out-of-control cells and loving them back into place is also a valid way to heal ourselves and others. If we see ourselves as connected to the entire universe, we will be able to see everything as part of our life. We do what we feel is needful to our healing, which might include surgery, medication, or alternative therapy to intervene and bring us back into balance. But ultimately embracing every part of ourselves and our being—not fighting it—keeps us whole and alive, even in the face of death.

THE JOURNEY CONTINUES

Brent was adamant about refusing chemotherapy. Although this technique was developed almost sixty years ago, not much progress has been made in its effectiveness. A *Wall Street Journal* article I read at the time pointed out that cancer continued to kill people at much the same rate as it had forty years previous. Chemotherapy remains a shotgun approach: kill off everything and maybe in the process you'll hit the cancer. There are no guarantees, and the side-effects can be debilitating.

In my search on the Internet, I found some new treatments that were less invasive than surgery. One was laser therapy. Using a laser, surgeons carve off the cancerous tissue without harming the good tissue surrounding it. It sounded like something Brent could live with: if he's going to die anyway, then let's choose the least invasive route. He agreed.

I began calling around to find a doctor who knew about laser therapy. On Saturday evening, my daughter, who works in the medical field, called me, excited about a TV commercial she had just seen for an innovative laser therapy treatment at the Virginia G. Piper Cancer Center in Scottsdale, Arizona. She gave me the phone number.

I called the center and inquired about laser therapy. I was connected with a scheduler, but unlike the scheduler at the first oncologist's office, this woman was kind, empathetic, and very helpful. She gave me the name and phone number of the radiation oncologist, who could give us more information.

"Now if you have any problems scheduling, call me back and I'll help you," she said in a kind voice. "We're here to help you."

I called that doctor and was again welcomed by a friendly voice. She set the appointment for the following week. She didn't even inquire about whether Brent had insurance.

It was the waiting that was most difficult, at least for me. I kept imagining that as we were waiting for appointments and opinions, the cancer inside Brent was getting bigger.

It did. The two procedures he had in September to stretch

his esophagus worked wonders for a few weeks. Now Brent's esophagus was starting to close off again. Eating was becoming increasingly difficult. He tried to eat lunch before our appointment with the oncologist, but it didn't work. He was plugged up. It was terrible to watch him struggle, not even being able to swallow his own saliva.

Dr. Nick Flores met with us, reviewed the pictures from the CT scan, then delivered the bad news: Brent wasn't a candidate for laser therapy. The tumor was too large. Laser therapy is more for smaller, thinner cancers. However, he felt that Brent had much better odds than the other doctors had given him, disagreeing with the 20 to 30 percent chance the two previous doctors had projected. The cancer had not, from the evidence of the CT scan, gone to any other organs. It appeared to be very localized, and so was a good candidate for surgery. Of course, there was the worry of whether the cancer had spread to the lymph nodes. That couldn't be judged until surgery and a pathology report. He had his staff set up an appointment with an excellent surgeon and made an appointment with another medical oncologist to confirm his opinion.

Brent saw the second medical oncologist, Dr. Susan Partyka, first. Dr. Partyka was a rather young woman, and entered the room wearing capri pants and a sweater. Always one for liking pretty women, Brent was immediately impressed. But what impressesed him even more about Dr. Partyka was her blunt, straightforward attitude. "You don't need me," she declared after looking at the CT scans. "This thing is localized and hasn't spread. Go get it cut out and be done with it."

Brent was amazed. It was the first time a doctor—especially one in the business of selling chemotherapy—had actually made a recommendation that made sense to him.

Later that week, Friday, November 1, Brent's sixtieth birthday, we met with the surgeon, Dr. Bruce Freedman. He liked what he saw. He said if things were as good as they looked on the CT scan, he would give Brent an 85 percent chance of surviving longer than five years. That was extremely encouraging—certainly better odds than medical websites give people with this type of cancer. It was a brief examination, but he didn't like the feel of a lymph node under Brent's right arm. "Let's schedule a biopsy on this next week; then if that's clean, we'll do surgery," he said.

* * *

After Brent's death, I spent a few years as a hospice volunteer. I've both seen and heard about people who were given only a few months to live without treatment but who lived for a year or even two years. One gentleman in his eighties, diagnosed with leukemia, decided to forgo treatment. He was told that without it, he would only live six months at most. He went home to die under hospice care. Two years later, he was still alive and doing fairly well. The follower of an esoteric teacher, he believed that your thoughts create your reality. It was his belief that he was okay and wasn't going to die, but he also believed that if he did die, that would be okay too. His willingness to embrace whatever came his way without worry about the future or fear of death gave him life.

I have come to believe that we are better off when we do not do battle with the disease, but rather embrace and accept whatever the path may bring, whether that's healing of the body's ills or death, which is also a sort of healing—perhaps the ultimate healing.

During the past century, we have been removed from the specter of death. Most people die in hospitals, nursing homes, or hospice facilities. Unlike our ancestors, we do not see death up close and personally, and that has, I believe, contributed to our fear of death. We no longer see it as a natural part of life, but as a terrible end; the battle to stay alive at all costs is lost.

Death is not losing the battle, as we are so prone to believe. In fact, it doesn't really matter how we die, only how we live. Death is at last winning at the great game of life! You've passed the test! Your mind and soul no longer need this body, so you get to move on to the next level of consciousness until you've integrated this life into all your other lifetimes of learning. Then you'll come back in a new body and begin another phase of progression. You win!

In her book *Start Where You Are*, Buddhist nun Pema Chödrön says that we should not be a "walking battleground." This feeling comes because, she says, "we have such strong feelings of good and evil, right and wrong. The truth is that good and bad coexist; sour and sweet coexist. They aren't really opposed to each other."

Life is duality. When we allow ourselves to label something as "bad" and be drawn into this idea that this should somehow entail a battle, we are pulled downward into the darkness. Can we really judge something as good or bad? Things just are. Life just is. It's neither good nor bad because we aren't in a position to judge. Maybe we are experiencing exactly what we need to elevate us spiritually, to give us enlightenment. Nothing is all good. Nothing is all bad. Out of those situations and circumstances that we judge to be bad come some really wonderful opportunities. And what we deem to be "good" can often result in some "bad" events. We can all remember times when we got what we wanted—a new car, a bigger house, a handsome or beautiful spouse who seemed to offer us a wonderfully happy life—only to find a few years later that what we thought would be the source of our happiness was the source of our suffering.

According to Pema Chödrön, learning to live with whatever means letting "opposites coexist, not trying to get rid of anything but just training and opening our eyes, ears, nostrils, taste buds, hearts, and minds wider and wider, nurturing the habit of opening to whatever is occurring, including our shutting down."

In other words, let go and let it be!

4

LIVING CONSCIOUSLY: WHAT IS CONSCIOUSNESS?

It is important to understand consciousness if we are to understand life and living and dying and death, for consciousness creates the reality that we experience. To learn to live consciously, with awareness of how all phenomena exist, is critical to understanding how we die. I have found the study of consciousness extremely engaging. My interest was piqued by Brent's death. Having observed the various levels of consciousness he seemed to be experiencing as he moved toward his transition and hearing his account of what he was seeing while experiencing these levels, I delved into the study of consciousness. What is consciousness? How many levels of consciousness can we operate on at a given period of time? What role does meditation play in consciousness and recognizing what consciousness is?

At a talk at a Science and Nonduality (SAND) conference, one speaker noted that consciousness is not something we have; it is what we *are*. It is one constant, ever present element. It is not something to be discovered but recognized. "Consciousness," said the speaker, is "fundamental and universal." We are all conscious beings having experiences. So why is understanding consciousness important to our experience of both living and dying? Because, the speaker said, "understanding consciousness is the key to the understanding of reality."

Some define it as "pure awareness." We do not *have* awareness; we *are* awareness! We have the nature of pure awareness. Timothy Freke and Peter Gandy tell us: "You are awareness witnessing a flow of experiences we call life." We are not conscious beings who are aware of the world around us; we are pure awareness, consciously creating through observation. That is very similar to what quantum physicists call the *observer effect*, which says that nothing exists until it is observed. Matter exists as both waves and particles. Observations collapses the waves into particles, which then become "things." Things are not here in the material universe, waiting for us to observe them; we make phenomena appear by our observation. As Buddhism tells us, everything is created in the mind by the mind. There is no reality outside of mind.

Freke and Gandy say that "if you become conscious of your essential nature as awareness you will see that you can't possibly die, because you were never born. You are awareness which witnesses the birth of the body and which will one day witness its death." Awareness "is a permanent presence" within consciousness that is continually arising. Awareness becomes one with what it is witnessing. Awareness bridges the gap of duality, the gap that lies between me over here and you over there. With pure awareness, the duality of physical existence ceases to exist, and the result is unity of consciousness.

Freke and Gandy explain that "awareness becomes conscious through these different forms [of physicality]. Consciousness is the relationship between awareness and a particular form it imagines itself to be in the life dream. . . . What awareness is conscious of through a particular form depends on the nature of the form." Consciousness, say these authors, "arises within the duality of the life dream."

We are never unconscious but are always conscious on some level—on planes that we do not apprehend with our waking minds. What science has recently discovered about consciousness; the Buddhists have known for many hundreds of years. The Buddhists preceded science by more than two millennia in understanding quantum consciousness and meditation's relationship to it. The purpose of meditation is to put us in touch with the various levels of consciousness and help us to understand that the level of consciousness we call "reality," or the "real world," is no more real than the experiences during sleep that we term "dreams." While our bodies rest, our souls move to other levels of consciousness, experiencing other places, other worlds, even other times, past or future—which really are not past or future, but always the present blended into one, eternal existence.

Meditation also moves us into the space that we experience in the dying process, teaching us not to fear that level of consciousness when we prepare to leave the physical body. Meditation enables us to experience the gap between the "here" and the "there" so that when we approach death, it will be comforting and familiar. The purpose of meditation is to help us know what is real and to separate it from the illusions that cloud our vision. As the Apostle Paul says, "We see through a glass darkly," meaning that we have no clarity of vision in our mortal bodies. Our vision in this body is clouded by the filters of our experiences and the five senses. Only our other, subtler bodies can see the real.

The Austrian esotericist Rudolf Steiner was an early student of consciousness. He sought to know "higher worlds" through what he termed "Christ consciousness" and wrote his book *How to Know Higher Worlds* to explain his understanding. Gary Lachman, in his book *A Secret History of Consciousness*, writes about Steiner's views:

> In a series of lectures on music given in Berlin in 1906, Steiner remarks that as the initiate proceeds in developing "supersensible perception" one of the signs of success is that his or her dream life changes. From the usual chaos of symbolic representations, the initiate enters a world of "flowing colors and radiant light beings." This, Steiner says, is the "astral world." Curiously, he remarks that the astral world is always present and surrounds us continuously, and that only the presence of our everyday consciousness prevents us from perceiving it.

Perhaps the illusions brought on by our sensory perceptions interfere with our ability to access the astral world. There are some who do have that ability, however, such as Allison DuBois, whose experiences became the basis for the television series *Medium*.

Seth, the entity channeled by Jane Roberts in the 1960s and early 1970s, advised that we need to develop this "supersensible perception," or the "Inner Senses," as he preferred to call it. Jane Roberts writes in her book *The Seth Material*: "The Inner Senses are not important because they release clairvoyant or telepathic abilities, but because they reveal to us our own independence from physical matter, and let us recognize our unique, individual multidimensional identity. Properly realized, they also show us the miracle of physical existence and our place in it."

In *The Nature of Personal Reality*, Seth tells Roberts, "The physical structure itself contains within it the necessary prerequisites for what you would call evolutions of consciousness—and even for, within certain limits, the organization of experience in ways that might seem quite alien to you now." He adds that "your consciousness is not a thing that you possess." That is true: consciousness is what we are. We are pure conscious awareness, which engages our experience and creates the reality of the material world.

We define *sentient beings* as beings that are aware. Higher beings, such as humans, are self-aware in that they possess the ability to be aware of an "I" in here that appears to exist separately from all other things in the world "out there." Seth is saying, again, that consciousness is not something that we happen to have because we have a body, a brain, or a mind, but rather we *are* consciousness. "Consciousness of self is still consciousness directly connected with action. Consciousness, therefore, is not a 'thing' in itself. It is a dimension of action, an almost miraculous state, made possible by what I call a series of creative dilemmas." We are not conscious because we exist in physicality; we exist in physicality because we are conscious.

Everything that we are, everyone we have ever been in all our so-called past lives (which Seth says are actually lived simultaneously), exists in consciousness. "In purely physical terms," Seth tells Roberts, "what you think of as consciousness of the self arises from a certain peak of intensity reached by the gestalt consciousness of the atoms and molecules, and cells and organs that compose the body."

What Seth says is the same thing that quantum physicists tell us today (and what the Buddha told people in 500 BCE): consciousness creates matter. Everything is created in the mind by the mind: nothing has any intrinsic existence. Not only does consciousness create matter, but everything that is created is created by mind or consciousness.

Lachman writes that no scientist has ever discovered consciousness by studying the physical hardware of the brain. He gives the example of making a "complete physical analysis of a compact disc containing Mozart's piano concertos" or of a copy of *War and Peace* "by breaking them down to their most basic elements, but in neither case would I approach the music or the novel. The surface of the compact disc and the ink and paper of the book are the means by which the music and the novel manifest; if I destroy them, I will only have destroyed one means of the music's and the novel's manifesting. . . . Both have their real existence in the consciousness of their creators, and once given to the world they now exist in a shared world of ideas which is also immaterial."

Although I once heard it said in a meditation class that heavy meditation results in a lack of a dream life, according to Steiner true development of perception, or "supersensible perception, "through deep meditation results in a more vibrant dream life, in which symbols dissolve into a new reality of consciousness. Part of this dream life occurs just at the onset of sleep. Known as hypnagogia, it is a state in which we can become aware of generally "unconscious" processes, such as dreams, while remaining conscious.

One of the most renowned students of this phenomenon is Andreas Mavromatis of London's Brunel University, author of *Hypnagogia: The Unique State of Consciousness between Wakefulness and Sleep*. More than simple daydreaming, hypnagogia is a state in which "we can 'see' sometimes utterly bizarre images and visions with an unsettling clarity, while remaining perfectly aware of the 'outside world.'" Mavromatis believed that it may have been in this state that Rudolf Steiner (as well as Edgar Cayce and others) claimed to read the Akashic Records. According to Lachman, hypnagogic states

> are almost always "auto-symbolic"—they represent either the physical or psychological states of the persons experiencing them, or their thoughts as they drifted out of consciousness. People experiencing hypnagogic hallucinations often shift in and out of "normal" sense of space and time. They see strange landscapes, and entire adventures can unfold in a few moments.
>
> Mavromatis points out that the thalamus, which he conjectures is the "center of consciousness" and the probable source of hypnagogia phenomena is anatomically linked to the reptilian brain (central core), limbic system (paleo-mammalian brain), and the cerebral hemispheres— the three "houses" of the "triune" human brain. . . . In

hypnagogia, he argues, the dominance of the cortex is inhibited through the onset of sleep, or through deep relaxation, allowing the "consciousness" of the other brains to appear. Usually, cortical consciousness is completely absent as we fall asleep, so we pass into these other states unawares. But if a minimum level of cortical arousal is maintained, then the consciousness of the old brain can be observed. This can be done, Mavromatis suggests, in meditative states which are characterized by the activation of the thalamus and other old-brain structures, and during which the practitioner is on guard against "falling asleep."

Mavromatis argues for the importance of the thalamus because it contains the pineal gland, which Descartes believed to be the seat of the soul. Lachman notes:

Dating back to the Devonian and Silurian periods, the pineal gland is extremely old. One of its earliest functions in primitive reptiles was as a kind of eye located in the top of the head, and in some contemporary vertebrates, including ourselves, the pineal gland is still photosensitive. In human beings the early "pineal eye" appears in the initial stages of embryonic life; it soon disappears, but its associated gland remains. And this, like the ancient eye, is sensitive to light. That the pineal gland is located precisely where ancient Vedic literature places the "third eye," whose function is "spiritual vision" and whose opening results in "enlightenment," offers some hard, neurological evidence for a belief too often relegated to fancy and superstition. . . .

Mavromatis remarks, "Hypnagogia gives rise to the insight that there are many realities and that what we call wakefulness merely constitutes one of them." . . . He goes on to suggest that our so-called waking state is hardly any less of a dream than the kind we experience during sleep. This, as hardly needs pointing out, is a perception shared by practically all mystical, occult, esoteric, and spiritual traditions. It is only in relatively recent times—taking place, perhaps not merely coincidentally, within the period Steiner calls the fifth post-Atlantean epoch—that our three-dimensional solid waking world has appropriated sole ownership of the category "reality."

B. Alan Wallace, president of the Santa Barbara Institute of Consciousness Studies, writes in *Tricycle* magazine that "Tibetan Buddhists formulated a system of teachings known as dream yoga over one thousand years ago that uses the power of lucid dreaming to break down our illusions and unlock the door to enlightenment. In dream yoga, once you learn to recognize the dream state for what it is through lucid dreaming, you can begin to explore the nature of the psyche—your own conscious mind within this lifetime."

Frank Zane, a three-time Mr. Olympia and competitive bodybuilder and trainer, talks about hypnagogia and the value of knowing the dream body in his practice. One night shortly after falling asleep, he heard the sound of a female voice, who told him that she was "the archetype of your unconscious mind" or Zane's "muse." She then explained that the dream body, although it "resembles your physique, it is not the same . . . and it is not subject to the laws of the physical world. You can go anywhere and accomplish anything in your dream body just by intending it." Zane's muse encourages people to visualize one's dream body "in the exact detail in which you wish to sculpt it."

Zane's muse explained how waking and dreaming life are interconnected. "Your waking life and your dreaming life run on a parallel course, and you will know you are progressing when you are able to become lucid in your dreams on a regular basis. As you learn to become more and more lucid in your dreams, you will learn to wake up during your 'waking' life as well," she said. "Your perception of the world is habitual, and you are too caught up in your physical existence. . . . The more lucid you become in your dreams, the more you will realize when you're awake that you are creating your entire world with your mind and your belief system."

Zane's muse then told him, "As you continue to practice over the years, your dream body will become as your physical body—so real that when you choose to relinquish your physical existence, your dream body will be your exit vehicle."

Seth tells Roberts that the dream state is a kind of short circuit of the neurological structures that allows us to

> perceive experiences of a multidimensional nature that you
> then attempt to translate, as best you can, into stimuli that
> can be physically assimilated—hence you often convert
> these into symbolic images that can be understood, and
> to some extent reacted to, by your bodily structure. . . .
> Your dream images are biologically structured, then. The
> experiences behind them bring you in contact with the

54

deepest portions of your nonphysical reality, and it is the unconscious who translates these for you into recognizable images and forms.

Death is much like deep sleep, the very subtle state that we experience before our consciousness rises to the less subtle REM stage. In fact, the Dalai Lama has explained that this deep sleep stage is as close to dying as we can get without actually dying. Falling asleep is often compared to dying in that we actually leave our body and move into another level or state of consciousness. Here, we are no longer aware of the self lying in bed sleeping, but of a self that is active and participating in another life—some say on a parallel universe—in order to give the physical body a rest.

In 2004, the Dalai Lama held the Mind and Life Conference at his home in Dharamshala, India. Participants, including several scientists, looked at consciousness in depth. Out of the conference was developed the book *Sleeping, Dreaming, and Dying: An Exploration of Consciousness*.

One of the participants, Jerome "Pete" Engel Jr., a professor of neurology at UCLA Medical School, referred to the book *Death, Intermediate State, and Rebirth in Tibetan Buddhism* by Lati Rinpoche and Jeffrey Hopkins, which, he said,

> explores the controversial idea of after-death experiences in the intermediate state following death and preceding rebirth, known as *bardo* in Tibetan.
>
> The book discusses stages of death which are then repeated in reverse order in the bardo state during the

transition towards rebirth. It says that sleep is in essence a rehearsal for this process of dying, and I was struck by the similarities between sleep and death.

The Dalai Lama answered,

> The experiences that you have while falling asleep and while dying result from the dissolution of the various elements. There are different ways in which this process of dissolution takes place. . . . The dissolution, or withdrawal, of the elements corresponds to levels of subtleties of consciousness. Whenever this dissolution occurs there is one common element: the differences in the subtlety of consciousness occur due to changes in the vital energies.

The Dalai Lama went on to observe that the aggregate of consciousness makes it seem as if

> consciousness, or mind, is a thing existing in and of itself. This is a false representation because there are many degrees of subtlety of consciousness. For example, the gross level of mind and energy exists in dependence upon the gross physical aggregates. As long as the brain is functioning, there is gross consciousness at this gross level. In the absence of a properly functioning brain, gross consciousness will not arise. So far, this Buddhist perspective accords with the neurosciences.

Robert Thurman, former Buddhist monk and author of *The Jewel Tree of Tibet: The Enlightenment Engine of Tibetan Buddhism*, expounds upon *The Tibetan Book of the Dead* by noting how narrow the space is between this life and the next, between being in this physical body and suddenly finding ourselves outside it. As "embodied" minds, we have become accustomed to operating within a physical body; after death we may retain the approximate shape of the physical body we have occupied for so many years and from which we exited. The only separation we experience is that of a fine line between what is physical and what is pure energy, existing in what might be called a virtual-reality state of being. Thus, says Thurman, there is no such thing as death as people normally think of it, and no such thing as nonexistence—or, as Thurman states, "Nobody stays dead; there are no dead people."

Jane Roberts's book *The Nature of Personal Reality* quotes Seth as saying, "A death is but one night to the soul."

Since all existence, including physicality, takes place in the mind, nothing ceases to exist at death. At the same time, nothing exists really: nothing inherently exists from its own side. We move from one type of existence to another. We are never *not* conscious, but rather are conscious on many levels. Truly, life is a mental continuum. This continuum contains all that we put into our minds throughout all our lifetimes; here, are planted the karmic seeds sown by everything we have ever done. The dream state is merely another existence, which we experience alongside physical existence, to give us additional information.

The thought struck me one morning, as I awoke from a

particularly vivid dream, that what I had just experienced was reality and this "awakening" was the dream. There is no separating one reality from another or one state of consciousness from another. It is all here. It is all so very near, or as Brent commented during one of his lucid dream states a few days before his death, "[Reality] is just right there—it's just right there!" he said, pointing outward, very close to his body. Perhaps it is that dying and dreaming are one and the same thing; all is consciousness.

Seth explains that consciousness "is not a 'thing' in itself. It is a dimension of action." It is also a state in which all things exist. "Know that within your physical atoms now the origins of all consciousness still sing and that all the human characteristics by which you know yourselves still exist."

Seth also says that we "have other conscious selves" that exist on various other planes of reality. These are similar to Dr. Stuart Hameroff's theory of the "superposition" of consciousness. Dr. Hameroff is an anesthesiologist and founder of the Center for Consciousness Studies at the University of Arizona's School of Medicine. He began his research after noticing that even when he put someone under anesthesia, they remained conscious on a level other than this one, sometimes to the point where they watched their own surgery from a corner of the room near the ceiling. Some would even go outside and watch what went on outside the hospital, describing in detail the weather, the ambulances coming and going, the patients being wheeled into the emergency room, and other goings-on.

Sri Nisargadatta Maharag, a guru who did not believe that

one needed an outside guru, only an internal one, put it quite simply: "You are consciousness represented by the body."

Perhaps we can put it even more simply: you are consciousness.

5

UNDERSTANDING CONSCIOUSNESS AND REALITY

Reality is widely debated in today's scientific and theological circles. In determining what is real we are brought to the point of understanding that there is a "realer" reality than the one we experience at the level of consciousness in which our five senses are involved. Our brain certainly plays a part in helping us to determine our reality, but what role does mind play? "The brain is the organ that discerns what is real," said Andrew Newberg in an interview for *What Is Enlightenment?* magazine. "This presents a slight problem for the materialist position because when people have mystical experiences, they universally report that they have experienced something that is *more real* than our everyday material reality. Which means that the brain perceives God, or pure consciousness, to be more real than anything else. So if the brain is what determines what is real and what isn't, and this is a universal experience of human brains across cultures, where does that leave us?"

Sri Nisargadatta said, "God may exist but only if there is an 'I' to perceive it. Without an I to perceive it, then who will confirm its existence?" Which leads to his next point: "If you want to see the truth you have to dissolve I AM to the question 'Who are you?'"

While the brain is the hardware that enables our five senses to work on this level of consciousness, the mind is a different entity—the software, one might say. The mind can work independently from the brain, and in fact often does work independently on various levels of consciousness, such as REM sleep. In this state, we experience dream activity, including interacting with people, talking, traveling, and seeing our environment—all with the eyes, ears, and mouth of the mind, not of the body. The same thing occurs for those people who have near-death or out-of-body experiences, in which they go somewhere in mind only. The mind can reveal to us a reality that we have difficulty understanding in our waking life when the physical brain and the senses are constantly at work.

It is difficult to define reality, because if, as the materialists say, reality consists of only what we can see, hear, touch, taste, and feel, that eliminates a whole spectrum of experience, such as the dream state, near-death experiences (NDEs), coma states, and anesthetized states. The hit cult movie, *What the (Bleep) Do You Know?* delved into this question. Quantum physics has shown that there is more reality out there than we can identify in waking consciousness.

Dr. Peter Russell studied mathematics and theoretical physics at Cambridge University, supervised for a time by Stephen Hawking. He became fascinated by the nature of consciousness and changed his major to experimental psychology. He has a postgraduate degree in computer science and did some early work on virtual reality and 3D imagery.

In a keynote speech given at the 2006 Science and Consciousness Symposium in Santa Fe, New Mexico, Russell urged that "being awake is critical in our world today." He added that while the "global brain is connecting up" through the Internet, what about global consciousness? "There is a crisis of consciousness, . . . of thinking," he said. "Too much thinking is limited, self-centered, me-first thinking that is not working."

Ken Wilber, in *The Spectrum of Consciousness,* points to the work of the French philosopher Henri Bergson regarding the "spurious reality of things": it is thought that produces or "creates things by slicing up reality into small bits that it can easily grasp. Thus, when you are thinking you are thing-ing. Thought does not report things, it *distorts* reality to *create* things, and as Bergson noted, 'in so doing it allows what is the very essence of the real to escape.'"

During the final week of Brent's life, I would often observe that he moved in and out of states of consciousness that resembled lucid dreaming. He could answer my questions about what he was seeing and doing and say what it was like on the level of consciousness he was occupying at any given moment. The reality he was experiencing, while not of the level in which we are awake and aware, was for him a vaster and more real level of consciousness. At times he was completely unaware of what was going on in the house around him or that the TV was on. He would often startle back into this reality, confused. "Am I dead yet?" he would ask. I would assure him that he was not dead, just moving in between levels of consciousness. It caused me to ask him one day just before he died, "Is this world we experience real or is there a realer reality over there?"

He smiled, raised his right hand, and, pointing with his index finger into the space just above his head, said, "No, this is reality." He even said to me once, when I had remarked how beautiful the world is after coming in from reading on the patio one morning, "Over there is more beautiful."

We must all learn to experience this "realer reality" that exists outside this realm of conscious reality that we call life.

One morning, awaking from a vivid dream, my inner voice asked me the question: "What if that dream is your real life, and *this*, which you think is your real life, is a dream?" Good question! And it is one that I keep exploring in my studies of consciousness. Yes, there is a greater, "realer" reality than this one. Meditation helps us access that reality and befriend those states that we call dreaming or dying.

In Buddhism, one reason to practice nonattachment in daily meditation is to make dying much easier. It's one thing for a person who is old or ill or disabled to be grateful for death. For those of us who are healthy, strong, and living great lives, the thought of dying is very painful. Even so, dying is a fact of life. Nonattachment helps us to be ready for that moment when, say, a car comes speeding through an intersection and slams into us, leaving us without our bodies in an instant.

A Buddhist adage says, "Reality exists only where our mind creates a focus." Quantum physicists would say it is that focus that causes the collapse of waves of potentiality into particles, thus creating matter. From what I have read and experienced from working with dying people, I have learned that they begin to experience a different reality: their focus on this level of consciousness begins pulling away, and they lose interest in the things that surround them here. The world becomes gray and murky as they begin to detach from these phenomena their minds have so creatively constructed all these years. Dying people are very much in the *now* moment. Perhaps that is why the now should be so important to us long before we start the dying process. It's our only reality.

We are always aware, always consciousness, and the two go hand-in-hand. Vasant Lad, founder of the Ayurvedic Institute of Albuquerque, New Mexico, said in his presentation at the 2006 Science and Consciousness Symposium that "awareness is expansive. We are born out of pure awareness but when awareness is confined in a brain it becomes consciousness and it is expanding this consciousness to awareness. . . . 'I am' is what we all have in common. I am present in everyone and everyone is present in me."

The brain, the processor of the information provided by the senses, fools us into believing that the senses and only the senses can detect reality, but the brain cannot entrap the mind. The mind exists not only outside the brain, but after the death of the physical brain. A neurosurgeon once said that never has he opened up a person's skull, entered their brain, and found an identity. The brain merely processes the information. The mind interprets that information culturally, theologically, socially in ways that are different for each individual, like the story of the blind men describing the elephant.

Amit Goswami, PhD, quantum physicist in residence at the Institute for Noetic Sciences, says in his book *Physics of the Soul: The Quantum Book of Living, Dying, Reincarnation, and Immortality* that human life centers around meaning.

> Computers process symbols, but the meaning of the symbols has to come from outside—the mind gives meaning to the symbols that the brain generates.
>
> The feelings behind the vital function of a living organism come from the vital body of consciousness. Consciousness maps the vital functions in the form of the various functional organs in the physical body of the organism using its vital body.
>
> Since only consciousness can inject meaning in the physical world, it makes sense to hypothesize that consciousness "writes" the meaningful mental programs in the brain. . . . Similarly, consciousness must use the mental body to create the mental "software" (the representations of the meanings that mind processes) in the brain.

Seth would add that our consciousness creates matter.

> We gave you mental images and upon these images you learned to form the world that you know. We gave you the pattern by which your physical selves are formed. We gave you the patterns, intricate, involved, and blessed, from which you form the reality of each physical thing you know.

> The minutest cell within your brain has been made from patterns of consciousness which we have given you. . . . We taught you to form the reality you know.

Dr. Giancarlo Rosati, a surgeon and physician in Parma, Italy, whom I met through the LinkedIn group Spirituality and Consciousness, presented five ideas in an online discussion about reality that I found interesting; they follow here, with my comments.

1. *"Reality depends on the observer."* Dr. Rosati is noting that we all see the world differently. Your reality and my reality are many times two different things. We might, for example, agree that we are both looking at a painting by Picasso, but I see a beautiful abstract work of art that has meaning for me, while you see a mess of shapes and colors that you find quite horrible and has no meaning whatsoever for you.

2. *"The universe we perceive is in our mind."* All that we observe is created in the mind, by the mind, or as Fred Alan Wolf, PhD, says: "There is no *out there*, out there."

3. *"All is interconnected and interdependent: all is One."* We are all a part of the divine All That Is; each of us contains a spark of light that comes from the Source as the many rays of sunlight come from the same sun.

4. *"Creation is a continuous process,"* as the late British astronomer Sir Fred Hoyle proposed. We create at every moment of every day; everything is a continuum of rising and falling away, or like a celluloid movie strip in which each frame

appears individually but when put into a projector and shown on the screen, appears to be a stream of motion as each frame arises and falls away rapidly.

5. *"The Absolute is a quantum space/void."* However, it is filled with "potential"—energy, perhaps—for all that the observer creates, collapsing the waves of potentiality into particles of actuality. There is no true "space," as the Kabbalists knew when they wrote that the Ain Sof (the No-thingness) had to "carve out" (*tzimtzum*) room in the void in order to create. The fundamental nuclear elements involved in creation are the neutrons, the protons, and the electrons (see the Trimurti: Brahma, Vishnu, and Shiva).

Physicist Ervin Laszlo, in his book *Science and the Akashic Field: An Integral Theory of Everything,* reminds us that we live in an *informed* universe:

> We are not just a block of cells, like a building is a block of bricks. Most fundamentally, our living tissue is not made of hard-core elements—atoms and molecules—it is made of waves. Thus, we are living systems that are continually receiving and transmitting information. This information transmission is faster than any conceivable biochemical mechanism because what happens in one part of the organism simultaneously happens to the other part. It's constantly interactive on multiple dimensions. It's a remarkable thing—going way beyond any technical, biological, mechanistic, and materialistic concept of the organism. . . .

Consciousness is not a byproduct of the brain, produced by a complex set of neurons. It's something that's pervading the whole universe. It's there in the whole body, in all living systems, probably all the way down to the quantum level. We are living in a universe that itself is conscious.

"Mind and intelligence are woven into the fabric of the Universe," says Dr. Stuart Hameroff. "What is the fabric of the Universe? The Universe does have an underlying structure." We can call that structure the web of the universe or the akashic field, but there is a structure. Perhaps it is in this underlying structure in which our consciousness resides and permits us to pop into various states that include waking consciousness, sleeping consciousness, dream consciousness, and anesthetically induced consciousness.

The late Rabbi Samuel M. Cohon, formerly of Temple Emanu-El in Tucson, Arizona, has worked with Hameroff on consciousness studies. Hameroff quoted the following excerpt from an article by Rabbi Cohon, "The Origins of Awareness," during a session at a Science and Consciousness conference at the University of Arizona.

> There is another theory of what it is that creates consciousness. It holds that consciousness is not the result of some meta-mechanical process that emerges when we have enough on/off switches working at once. It is not the result of a massive collection of binary bits that spontaneously combust into awareness. It suggests that instead consciousness is fundamental to the universe, that the components

of our own self-awareness are present in the smallest elements of existence. That, in fact, everything in the world has a latent potential for consciousness, but that we humans are blessed with a higher level of those elements— and the sensory apparatus to bring them to life—that make for a complex sense of identity. This theory holds that consciousness is part of the fabric of space-time, the very material of creation of all existence.

"All is rooted in consciousness," says Theosophist Joy Mills. "Consciousness is truth and right bearing."

Seth agrees: "Consciousness creates matter," not the other way around. Matter does not exist, so that we can be conscious of it; rather we create matter through conscious awareness of all that is.

Consciousness doesn't just come from somewhere outside us. It arises on a moment-by-moment basis. We *are* consciousness. We experience that consciousness in mind, where the continuity of consciousness resides and remains with us for eternity. All is consciousness: plants, insects, even rocks and minerals. All is consciousness experiencing—*creating*—the physical plane through the integration of mind and brain. According to Buddhist teaching, consciousness is the ultimate creative principle.

All phenomena are a construct of the mind. Your mind creates your own reality; your conscious mind creates all that is, but this phenomenal world is empty of inherent existence. Buddhism agrees, teaching that all phenomena is created in the mind by the mind; nothing exists inherently from its own side. This world does not exist at a specific point in time and space, waiting for us to land physically upon it. Rather, we create this world and everything we see, hear, touch, taste, and smell through the senses and the mind. What we experience in physicality—what we see, hear, feel, taste, touch, and smell—is mutable and impermanent; it has no permanent, inherent existence or intrinsic nature. This is known as "conditioned reality" in *The Secret Doctrine* by H.P. Blavatsky. In Buddhism, it is also known as "conceptual reality," or "conventional truth," as opposed to "ultimate truth" or "unconditioned reality." It is also known as the law of dependent co-arising or dependent origination, because the phenomenal world exists in dependence upon an observer. Conditioned reality is the reality created by our minds when all the conditions for creating the phenomena are right. Take a rainbow, for example. A rainbow is an example of a conditioned reality because it manifests when all the necessary conditions are present: moisture in the atmosphere, direction of the sunlight to allow the refraction of light and water vapor, and of course the all-important observer to observe (create?) the rainbow. One could say that a rainbow is an illusion created in and by the mind of the observer and mistaken for reality.

Plato taught that this world that we perceive is a gross illusion. To illustrate this, he told his story of the cave. A man sat chained his entire life facing a cave wall. There was a fire burning behind him, and he could only see the shadows of those who moved back and forth behind him, not the actual physical people. To that man, the shadows on the cave wall were real.

Plato's point was that what we are apprehending on this level of consciousness with our gross minds are merely shadows, not reality.

Plato argued for a world of transcendent forms. In addition to the phenomenal world—the material world of sensation— Plato believed in a transcendent world of absolute, perfect, unchanging, ideal forms or eternal essences, apart from the things of which they were the causes.

Similarly, in Buddhism, there is the material, phenomenal world, which is called the *desire realm*. The *form realms* are different in that here, although there is form, it is recognized as emptiness. As the Buddhist sutra says, "Form is emptiness; emptiness is form." Thus, the Buddha's form realm may be the same realm that Plato would speak of some three hundred years later. This in turn would resemble the Hermetic philosophy of "as above, so below," in which the reality of this material world is a mere copy of a higher realm above.

An illusion is a distortion of a sensory perception, or a distortion of perceived reality—maya. *Maya*, in the Eastern traditions, is a polyvalent term. Maya is the principal deity who creates, perpetuates, and governs the phantasmagorical phenomenal world. What our senses perceive in waking consciousness is very real as conditioned reality, again because the conditions are right for us as observers to perceive it. But this reality is fleeting. For example, when the physical body falls asleep, the mind creates another reality—the dream state— which at that point is just as real to us as our waking consciousness is. *Ahamkar* (ego consciousness) and karma are seen as part of the binding forces of maya. The *samskaras* of perceived duality perpetuates samsara, or the rounds of birth, death, and rebirth, for many lifetimes.

According to the Hindu Advaita Vedanta philosophy, Maya covers Vishnu's eyes in *yoga nidra* (divine sleep) during the cycles of existence when all is resolved into one. Maya is the lesser reality that must be overcome so that one is able to realize the true Self. Maya, the purely physical and mental in which our everyday consciousness has become entangled, is the source of duality. In the Upanishads it says, "Maya is neither true nor untrue. Since Brahman is the only truth, Maya cannot be true. Since Maya causes the material world to be seen, it cannot be untrue."

H.P. Blavatsky writes in *The Secret Doctrine* that cosmic ideation can only occur if there is an observer. No cosmic ideation took place during periods of *pralaya* (universal rest) because that there was no one "to perceive its efforts." Blavatsky goes on to say, "As matter existing apart from perception is a mere abstraction, both aspects of Absolute—Cosmic Substance and Cosmic Ideation—are mutually interdependent. . . . the term 'Matter' ought to be applied to the aggregate of objects of possible perception, and 'Substance' to noumena; for inasmuch as the phenomena of *our* plane are the creation of the perceiving Ego." In other words, perception, or consciousness, that is, mind, creates matter.

The Buddhist law of dependent origination, or co-arising, holds that nothing exists apart from or independent of the perceiver; all phenomenal things depend upon, or co-arise with, a conscious observer. The consciousness "dependently co-arises with awareness," says Goswami. "In the quantum theory of the self, the atman [cosmic-consciousness experience] is seen as the quantum self—the unconditional universal subject with which consciousness identifies and that arises co-dependently with awareness upon the collapse of the quantum coherent superposition."

The typical idea of what Martin Heidegger calls *Being-in-the-world* would indicate that the world is separate and exists inherently in physical reality apart from the observer. In fact, rather than Being-in-the-world, we are continually creating the world in which we are observers, creators, and experiencers. Heidegger defines the Greek word *physis, nature,* as "a spontaneous coming into the light of being from a place of darkness." Physis, explains Heidegger, "requires that one adjust to the emergence of things in their own time and of their own accord, and make provisions for their inevitable withdrawal."

All things are in rhythm—arising and falling away, emerging and withdrawing. Heidegger says, "Truth (*aletheia*) follows the rhythm of emergence and withdrawal," adding that "technological thinking imperils Dasein . . . by promoting a truncated understanding of beings." He goes on to say that "Our task is to ready ourselves to receive the saving power by practicing technological asceticism, reserving for ourselves the freedom to say no to technology."

In *Echoes from the Gnosis,* author G.R.S. Mead, commenting on the Hymns of Hermes, says:

> The Greek equivalent of *maya* is *phantasia*, which, for lack of a single term in English to represent it rightly, I have

translated by "thinking manifest." The Phantasy of God
is thus the Power (Shakti in Sanskrit) of perpetual self-
manifestation or self-imagining, and is the means whereby
all "This" comes into existence from the unmanifest
"That"; or as our treatise phrases it:

"He is Himself, both things that are and things that are
not. The things that are He hath made manifest, He keep-
eth things that are not in Himself."

When someone dies, we say they are no longer manifest: they
are no longer available to be apprehended by our five senses.
They have moved to the realm of the unmanifest, where only
other mind forms can apprehend them.

In Buddhism there are three forms of mind. Maya creates
the delusions of the *gross mind*, or waking consciousness. The
gross mind, the sensory mind, depends upon the five senses,
which create illusions. The *subtle mind* is the mind of dreaming
and death, when the deluded mind drops away and we know
that there is no inherent reality in any phenomenal objects. The
very subtle mind is the mind that endures after the death process is complete. Also called the *clear light* or *emptiness mind*, it
resides in the *bardo* state until rebirth.

The Dalai Lama pointed out that death occurs when the
body is no longer able to support consciousness, that is, the
gross mind. Or, to look at it from Seth's viewpoint, death
occurs when the consciousness is no longer able to support the
physical body, given that consciousness creates matter. Amit
Goswami tells us in *Physics of the Soul*:

Death is the withdrawal of these identifications [with organs, the brain, our gross physical bodies as a whole]. With science within consciousness, we can say that the withdrawal of identification coincides with consciousness ceasing to collapse the quantum possibilities arising in the various components of the complex organism. This is a gradual process; consciousness withdraws first from the brain, then from the organs (although this ordering is sometimes reversed), and finally from the individual cells. For all practical purposes, a person is dead when consciousness ceases to identify with its brain.

People in the process of dying often experience both the gross mind and the subtle mind. This can cause confusion about what level of consciousness they are occupying. It is like waking up from a dream that seemed so real that you were confused about whether you were in your own bed or in some other place. Dying people experience the higher states of reality, in which the gross mind begins to fall away, and the subtle mind of the dream state takes over. The illusions of this level of consciousness that we term "reality" become increasingly apparent.

6

MIND, CONSCIOUSNESS, AND CREATION

"The conscious mind allows you to look outward into the physical universe, and see the reflection of your spiritual activity, to perceive and assess your individual and joint creations," Seth says. "Your joy, vitality and accomplishments do not come from the outside of you as the results of events that happen *to* you," he continues, but rather they "spring from inner events that are the result of your beliefs." (Seth uses the term "conscious Mind," but I'd rather say that mind *is* consciousness; consciousness is the function of mind.)

Seth explains that "Mind is physically directed, utilizes the greatest sources of power and energy along with unlimited aspects of creativity, so that each physical day is absolutely unique. "Mind does move Matter," says Seth, which would explain why Jesus said, "If you have faith, you can move mountains."

"In your terms," Seth continues, "consciousness is wedded with matter."

Consciousness affects matter, and observation of phenomena by a conscious observer affects reality. Quantum physics posits the *observer effect*, whereby the mere observation of phenomena—even passive observation—can change the phenomena. Scientists have discovered that the act of observing can actually change the measured result of the test. Thus, while the physical world appears to be made of solid stuff in a separate existence from us and everything else and is just waiting for us to see it, that isn't true. All phenomena exist as waves of potentiality or possibility awaiting an observer at which point the waves of potentiality collapse into actuality; the observer is the creator. The world and all in the world including ourselves cannot be as they appear to be—solid, real, and permanent. Ernest Holmes says in his primary work, *The Science of Mind*, that

> man's ignorance of his real nature binds him with his own freedom, until he comes to see things as they really are, and not as they appear to be. "Thought Force" (which some might call *will*) creates the movement of consciousness in a field of mechanical but intelligent law. The movement of consciousness upon itself creates a motion or vibration upon matter. To have an objective world, there must be a subjective observer. . . .We have Creative Intelligence at our disposal. The Universal subjective mind, being entirely receptive to our thought, is compelled by its very nature, to accept that thought and act upon it no matter what the thought may be. . . . Man's self-knowing mind is the instrument which perceives Reality and cognizes or realizes Truth. Nothing could give form to formless stuff, which has no mind of its own, but some intelligence operating through it.

Holmes also says that mind is the creator of all we experience. He quotes the philosopher Immanuel Kant: "We are able to perceive an object because it awakens an intuitive perception within us. How could it awaken an *intuitive perception* within us, unless the medium which created the object already existed within us? The intuitive perception was not the *result* of perceiving the object but *was itself the cause of the object perceived*! This is what Emerson would have us understand when he says, 'There is one mind common to all individual men.'" Holmes writes:

> The perception and the perceiver must be in one and the same Mind. *No object can appear to exist in the objective world unless there is first a subject world to perceive the object.* There is no object on the *outside* of Reality; but Reality must be an Infinite Perceiver or an Infinite Mind.
>
> Images of thought, although they appear to arise from without, *actually arise from the objective side of that which is part of a subjective within.* . . . there must be an objective, a manifest world; but that which is physically outside of us still exists in the same medium in which we have our being, and the intelligence by which we perceive it is the SAME INTELLIGENCE THAT CREATED IT. (Emphasis Holmes's)

Mind makes sentience, or the higher level of consciousness that humans and animals enjoy (with humans also having an experience of a separate self). Matter is consciousness on a lower level because all matter is consciousness in one form or another. Scientists point out that every cell of our body has its own individual consciousness, which enables it to respond to thought, instruction, and perception. Even plants are conscious, as experiments have shown them to respond more positively to beautiful music than to heavy-metal music.

The Yoga Vasistha states: "The body does not create the mind, but the mind the body. The mind is the seed of the body. If the body perishes, the mind can create other bodies." The mind-healing movement that began to attract popular attention in the United States during the 1800s was an outgrowth of the Eastern philosophy of mind as creator of all things, including our bodies: the mind controls the state of our body. Mind healing became a leading alternative to allopathic treatment.

Physicist Erwin Schrödinger, famous for his paradoxical cat in the box theory, said, "The external world and consciousness are one and the same thing." In other words, consciousness creates the world of experience.

Arthur Stanley Eddington (1882–1944), a British astronomer, physicist, and mathematician, commented in his book *The Nature of the Physical World*, "The stuff of the world is mind stuff." Eddington argued, "Mechanical theories of the ether and of the behavior of fundamental particles have been discarded in both relativity and quantum physics." Furthermore, "all we know of the objective world is its structure, and the structure of the objective world is precisely mirrored in our own consciousness. We therefore have no reason to doubt that the objective world too is 'mind stuff.' Dualistic metaphysics then cannot be evidentially supported."

Eddington went on to argue, "Not only can we not know that the objective world is nonmaterialistic, we also cannot intelligibly suppose that it could be material. To conceive of a dualism entails attributing material properties to the objective world. However, this presupposes that we could observe that the objective world has material properties. But this is absurd, for whatever is observed must ultimately be the content of our consciousness, and consequently, nonmaterial."

Universal Consciousness—which, as H.P. Blavatsky notes in *The Secret Doctrine*, has seven levels into which humankind can tap—pervades all beings, sentient and nonsentient. The physical world that we experience is the level of maya or illusion. Only the ultimate Reality (emptiness) is real. It can be experienced in the higher states of meditation or in states of what is called *cosmic consciousness*.

Mind creates reality at the level of consciousness upon which it operates. Universal Consciousness creates the universe by *becoming* it through a series of contractions. Growing less and less subtle, it gradually becomes more and more gross as it descends into physicality (solid matter). On its way, it becomes mind and the five senses and organs of action. This is the Fall that all spiritual traditions speak of. The Fall from light into darkness; from clarity into illusion or maya; from the unmanifest to the manifest. God creates from itself: part of itself remains in each mind as an eternal spark—seer, witness, indweller, Self—animating and imbuing it with the life force—the vital energy, the *élan vital*.

Ultimately, we live in an informed universe. Information pervades the cosmos, which, as Peter Russell says, "is an aware field of Being." The brain's job is to process this information, and how our brain processes this information "affects what appears in consciousness. . . . Form appears in consciousness."

Consciousness also acts as a witness to the physical world. Brian Hodgkinson, in his excellent commentary *The Essence of Vedanta,* talks about the various states of mind (waking, deep sleep, and REM sleep) and the creation of the reality that exists in these states, noting that "none of these states, individual or universal, are consciousness. They are simply states of the intellect (*buddhi*). Consciousness itself is the one, undifferentiated, ever constant, self-validating, self-conscious presence in all three states. It is the witness of whatever state the intelligence undergoes."

Hodgkinson warns us about confusing the witnessing subject with the object witnessed, "lest the idea of a witness is taken to imply a duality between witnessing subject and witnessed objects. The Mandukya [Upanishad] reminds us that the whole phenomenal world represented by the three states is in reality negated when the truth about pure consciousness is realized." When one realizes that the entire phenomenal world is created by our conscious awareness, one understands the illusion of physicality.

In the Kabbalah, the Ain Sof (literally *no limit* or the *infinite)* creates (or rather differentiates itself) from the potential that exists in the universe, from which the observer creates all it observes. Ain Sof is nonduality, *no-thingness.* When the Ain Sof differentiates the potential (the light and energy), *no-thingness* becomes *thingness:* it takes on a dualistic appearance. That is the "me in here" and the "you out there."

Heidegger writes, "Logic fails utterly before the horrific and unthinkable convergence of nothingness and being. The horizon of beings, the condition of the possibility of the totality of things that are and could be, is not substance or act but nothingness." Perhaps he is speaking of an undifferentiated "no-thingness" or nonduality prior to the creator—whether that is some God or Divine Mind or even ourselves as observers—differentiating and thus creating *things*, or duality. Enlightenment is the act of moving from duality to nonduality (unity). It moves beyond things as we know them to no-things—no more "me in here" and "you out there."

Thomas Aquinas spoke of the *actus purus* or "the fullness, not emptiness, an infinite plenum that grounds and makes possible the reality of particular beings." The void of the universe, spoken of in Genesis 1:2, was filled with this plenum, which is the ground of being from which all things are created or become differentiated. So much so that according to Kabbalistic teachings, the Creator—the Ain Sof—had to perform the act of *tzimtzum*, literally a "withdrawal," in order to make room for its creation. This void may be what we today call *dark matter* or *dark energy*; or perhaps we can even call it pure consciousness—the root of all creation.

7

THE WITNESS:
OBSERVER OF ALL

What happens when we act as a witness? We see an event taking place; we can confirm that the event took place because we have used our senses to confirm it. We can tell others what happened, and thus it becomes "reality."

We can also witness an even deeper reality—that of the Absolute Subjectivity or the Witness within each of us, as the theologian Paul Tillich observes: "We take the word God to mean 'depth,' and this 'depth' is exactly that Absolute Subjectivity or Witness within each of us, identified with neither subject nor object, but paradoxically including both."

In *The Spectrum of Consciousness*, Ken Wilber says that Sri Ramana Maharshi defines the Witness thus: "Since the Self, which is pure Consciousness, cognizes everything, it is the Ultimate Seer [Absolute Subjectivity]." Wilber notes that the Hindu philosopher Shankara elaborates upon this Absolute Subjectivity: "Now I shall tell you the nature of this Absolute Witness. If you recognize it, you will be freed from the bonds of ignorance, and attain liberation. We have been witnesses from the beginning of time; witnesses and observer/creators of each of our lifetimes throughout eternity, made possible by our nature of pure awareness."

In *The Laughing Jesus,* Timothy Freke and Peter Gandy say, "If you become conscious of your essential nature as awareness you will see that you can't possibly die, because you were never born. You are awareness which witnesses the birth of the body and which will one day witness its death."

It reminds me of the little book by Richard Bach, *There's No Such Place as Far Away,* in which he is flying to a party to celebrate little Rae's birthday. Along the way he speaks to many birds, who ask where he is going. When Eagle asks, he replies that he is going to a birthday party. The eagle says, "I understand very little of what you say, but least of all do I understand this word *birthday.*"

"'Of course, birthday,' I said. 'We are going to celebrate the hour that Rae began, and before which she was not. What is so hard to understand about that?'" Eagle asks,

> "A time before Rae's life began? Don't you think rather that it is Rae's life that began before time ever was? You have no birthday because you have always lived; you were never born, and never will you die. You are not the child of the people you call mother and father, but their fellow-adventurer on a bright journey to understand the things that are."

Shankara says,

> There is a self-existent Reality, which is the basis of our consciousness of ego. That Reality is the Witness of the

states of ego consciousness and the bodily coverings. That Reality is the Knower in all states of consciousness—waking, dreaming, and dreamless sleep. It is aware of the presence of absence of the mind and its functions. It is your real Self. That Reality pervades this Universe, but no one penetrates it. It alone shines. The universe shines with its reflected light. Because of its presence, the body, senses, mind, and intellect apply themselves to their respective functions, as though obeying its command.

Its nature is eternal Mind. It knows all things, from the ego to the body. It is the Knower of pleasure and pain and of the sense-objects. This is your real Self, the Supreme Being, the Ancient. It never ceases to experience infinite joy. It is always the same. It is Mind itself.

Shankara is explaining that the Witness is the Knower—the real Self or the Higher Self that transcends the lower self or the ego. Absolute Subjectivity or the Witness, says Wilber, is "nondual consciousness"—or unity with All That Is. At the point at which we experience nondual consciousness, we experience Mind in its purest form in which the "I" and the "thou" no longer exist but only the *tathagata* or the "suchness" of being.

At that point, we might experience what Wilber calls the "supra-individual Witness": "that which is capable of observing the flow of what is—without interfering with it, commenting on it, or in any way manipulating it." That is what I have termed *God Mind*. God does not interfere with its creation, but rather observes it, acts as a witness to all that goes on in this space-time continuum. People who believe in an anthropomorphic God often become discouraged when tragedies and natural disasters occur in which many people are killed. They wonder why God didn't interfere. Surely an omnipotent, omniscient God *knew* of the coming disaster and the impending doom that would befall all those people. Volcanoes, earthquakes, floods, tsunamis, and other natural disasters seem to have been preventable by God. Instead, God just watches the movie. That's God Mind.

Many times, we as parents must have God Mind in dealing with our children. Certainly, we could rescue them from their mistakes and all the things that could befall them. When they are small, we often do for example, we rescue them from walking out into the street, where they may be hit by a car. We try to protect them from the things they do not know are dangerous until they are old enough to recognize danger. But when they become teenagers and young adults, they often make decisions on their own, for which there are consequences. Perhaps we should not save them from these. They create their karma and reap the consequences of their actions. We might take a perspective of God Mind, knowing that if we interfere, they may not experience what they need to experience in order to progress. We must withdraw the immediate emotion of wanting to save them (which arises from the ego) and instead allow their karma to play out.

In a Buddhist class one Sunday morning, we performed a meditation called "like a rock, like a stone," in which we visualized withdrawing all emotion, all feeling of attachment, all judgments, and merely observed the contents of our minds and our thoughts. It was a practice in being the Witness—just being the observer, as someone might be when watching a movie.

As the movie plays out, we watch it, realizing that we have no true knowledge of the actors; nor can we jump into the movie and change the outcomes. We might feel emotion—empathy with the protagonist or repulsion for the antagonist— but we understand that it doesn't really matter what we feel, because we can't have any effect on the movie or the characters.

Wilber notes that "the Witness simply observes the stream of events both inside and outside the mind-body in a creatively detached fashion, since, in fact, the Witness is not exclusively identified with either." Like when we watch a movie without identifying with the characters, we watch the mind objectively, merely witnessing the events on the mental screen before us. "When the individual realizes that his mind and his body can be perceived objectively," says Wilber, "he spontaneously realizes that they cannot constitute a real subjective self."

Witnessing involves being—being the observer of our thoughts and experiences. Freke and Gandy write, "It is disengaging from your apparent nature as a body, as Plotinus puts it, and recognizing that you are the spacious emptiness of awareness within which the life-dream is arising. Witnessing is transcending your separate self by being awareness which contains the world."

The Witness (subject) versus the witnessed (object) is the dualism from which we need to free ourselves if we are to realize Ultimate Mind. The seer is never different from the seen: the knower of this phenomenal field—*purusha,* or pure consciousness, in Sanskrit—is never different from what can be known of this phenomenal field—*prakriti* in Sanskrit. For it is all one great unity of mind; all is created in mind.

Hugh Brockwell Ripman, a follower of the spiritual teacher G.I. Gurdjieff, speaks of the Silent Witness: "The Silent Witness pays attention to what goes on in the centers: to what goes on in the head, to what goes on in the heart, to what goes on in the body. "In other words, the Silent Witness is the Observer that stands alone watching, paying close attention to every aspect of the Self, including the mind, the body, and the emotions. Ripman writes:

> It is simply being aware as though each function had a mirror placed in front of it. . . . The thing to do is to experience the Silent Witness. . . . We're all trying to do the same thing, to have a Silent Witness whose function is just to be aware . . . to find how it feels different from the ordinary condition when your thoughts are experienced as "I," when your feelings are experienced as "I," when your body is experienced as "I." . . . What is important is to know the difference in oneself between the times when it's there and the times when it's not. . . . What matters is that you experience it.

Ripman emphasizes that experiencing the Silent Witness isn't a "thinking effort," because the minute you think about it, you're not the Witness, but merely the thinker. Witnessing involves stepping back—being both the observer and the observed without attachment to the action or the outcomes, much as one watches a movie. It resembles hypnagogia as one is falling asleep or waking up, when one makes that subtle transition from the thinker—the subject of thought—to the object that one is observing. The gap that separates the two is no longer there, and one knows that the seer and the seen are unified.

In that state one is dispassionately observing what is being said or done without judgment or thought. It is an observation of the self without any attachment to the self because it no longer exists as a separate entity. "One is simply seeing, in relation to this process of observing oneself, what goes on the whole time when one is observing other people and things: one is constantly (and cannot help it) interpreting and analyzing," Ripman explains. "When we try to observe ourselves directly, then it is almost impossible to prevent some kind of feeling or thought about what we observe from arising in us; but one has to keep the feeling or thought about what we observe quite separate from the act of observation." After all, isn't that what being a witness really encompasses?

Rajendranath Mehrotra, an online friend from India, writes:

> If we remain trapped in our own thoughts, we will not have control over them. When we start to observe them, we separate ourselves from them and we provide a space. This is how we can control them and channel them in the direction we wish.
>
> In order to have control over something we must look at it from a certain distance, like an impartial observer. This practice helps us to realize the influences, both positive and negative, that there are in our life. Observing our thoughts (which we do in the process of meditation) is the first step in understanding and, in the last analysis, taking full responsibility for them.

This stepping back, of putting space between our thoughts (which arise from the ego) and the observations we make independently of our thoughts, is moving beyond the ego to a position of witnessing. Benedictine monk Bede Griffiths notes:

> In meditation one tries to calm the body and the senses, to calm the mind, and become what's called "the silent witness," the witness beyond the mind. We in the West think that the mind is everything, but all Eastern practice is to get beyond the mind to the point of the silent witness, where you're witnessing yourself, where you've gone beyond the ego, beyond the self.

Meditation isn't about emptying the mind and thinking about nothing. On this human level of consciousness, it is impossible to eliminate all thoughts from our mind. The purpose of meditation is to tame the mind by observing the thoughts that arise and allowing them to fall away so that we do not become driven by them but instead become the Witness of all that we are thinking.

Bruce Rosenblum and Fred Kuttner discuss in depth the world of quantum "waviness" and "particles" and how observation and measurement influences the behavior of atoms. "We seem to be saying that somehow observing an atom being at a particular place created its being there. . . . Observations not only *disturb* what is to be measured, they produce it." This would indicate that mind is the creator of what we call the "objective" observable world; we are not just observing something that is already "out there" awaiting an observer but actually creating as we are observing.

We are the witnesses to creation as well as the creators of what we witness. In many cases, police will interview a number of witnesses to a crime, and each one will describe something different: each saw the event in a slightly different way, each creating a unique event in their minds. As the Witness to our life's experiences and as the Observer of all that we create, we come to that peak experience of unity—of impartiality, non-attachment to outcomes, and freedom from judgment that is critical to letting go and experiencing Be-ness. We develop the absolute subjectivity that allows us to *be* and releases us from the burden of trying to intervene in our thoughts. Instead, we allow the "movie" to play out—to be what it will be with non-attachment, which brings equanimity and peace.

8

ATTACHMENT, LOSS, AND THE LIBERATION OF NONATTACHMENT

I once read that all fear is rooted in the fear of loss. We all feel a sense of loss when someone or something we love disappears from our life. The loss of a loved one—especially in death—leaves us feeling sad, lonely, and often fearful of what life holds now that the person is gone. Natural disasters often cause the loss of our material possessions, which can also leave us feeling empty and afraid as we ponder how to pick up the pieces and take the next step. Our material existence is often grounded in the things and people we are attached to, and the loss we feel is a very human characteristic. How can we overcome this fear and all the emotions that grip us when loss occurs, especially to death?

From an Eastern philosophical standpoint, the practice of nonattachment is key to the acceptance of loss and dealing with emotions that come with it. Nonattachment is perhaps the least understood of all the Eastern spiritual concepts. Some confuse it with unattachment or detachment, but they are not quite the same thing. To be unattached or detached is to have had no connection at all, to break away from completely, or to have something broken away. By contrast, nonattachment indicates that a connection exists, but that one has made a choice to not attach oneself to the people or things involved.

According to Mahayana Buddhism, nonattachment is a mental factor that opposes attachment; it remedies a state of mind that has been brought on by mistaken appearances. These happen when we believe that the things we see, hear, and touch are inherently real. Attachment to the things we see brings on feelings of desire that bind us to samsara. Nonattachment liberates us from these mistaken appearances.

Many of us feel trapped in our lives; we feel as if we have no freedom or that we are controlled by external circumstances. Attachment permeates our lives. As a Buddhist teacher of mine, Kadam Michelle, once said, "We have a lot of attachments—some of which we may not even be aware—and are controlled by our attachments. How is this? There are pleasant, unpleasant, and neutral feelings. The pleasant feelings generate attachment. We like things a certain way and we don't recognize how deeply attached we are to these things in Samsara that generate these feelings. We externalize our sources of happiness. We see things as inherently existent and then desire it, and if we get what we desire, we become attached to it because we see it as inherent to our happiness."

However, we can also become attached to negative circumstances, even to our suffering. Physicist and spiritual teacher Ravi Ravindra points out that we can become attached to our suffering even more than to our happiness; otherwise, we wouldn't keep doing things that result in suffering. (It's like that definition of insanity: doing the same things over and over and expecting different results.) "Suffering stays more strongly in our psyches," Ravindra says. "We're attached to suffering—which is our root problem. Yoga is breaking the bond with suffering."

Many believe that people who practice nonattachment are cold, remote, distant, unemotional, and uncaring. Nothing could be farther from the truth. Nonattachment creates a greater sense of caring, a greater compassion, by removing the emotions of the ego from the equation. We become attached to people and things because there is an element of the "I" or self-grasping in the attachment. When "I" or "me" or "my" enters the picture, we are attached, because it is suddenly about "me." That attachment creates the delusion that there is some inherent, solid reality or permanence to the person or thing, or that we can control the outcome of an event. That attachment is the root of suffering.

Nonattachment provides us with the freedom to be loving, caring, and compassionate without regard to the "I," "me," or "my" feelings, wants, desires, hopes, or outcomes. We can be entirely compassionate without being pulled into the drama. We must realize that each person is operating within the framework of his or her own karma. Karmic seeds planted in the mental continuum, or the monad, over many lifetimes since beginningless time, ripen at various stages and in various lifetimes. We must understand that whatever is happening in a person's life is the result of this process: the karma is burned off so that the person can progress spiritually toward enlightenment. That is why, while I feel compassion toward all sentient beings and try my best to help them—to feed the hungry, to help the sick, visit the lonely, and lift the sad—I cannot save them from the implications of their karma. Therefore, I must not become attached to happiness or to sadness. This practice also leads to equanimity. The Bhagavad Gita says:

> Self-possessed, resolute, act
> Without any thought of results,
> Open to success or failure.
> This equanimity is yoga.

We must be in possession of our emotions and ego and must be resolute in our actions, but we must engage in our duty and act without any thought of results. We must be in control of our mind and train it so that we do what we do with the right intention. If we enter into action with an eye on results, or with wrong intention, we will not be free to act in the best interest of others—and that is the ultimate reason to act. Attachment to results distracts us from acting in the optimum manner to act on behalf of all sentient beings.

Nonattachment also allows us to be "open to success or failure." Not all of our actions will be successful, and everyone in this samsaric existence experiences failure. But as long as we are not focused on results, we can act with equanimity.

Nonattachment does not excuse us from our duty or from performing right action. As the Gita tells us, we must act; we must do our duty, but we cannot be attached to the outcomes of our actions. We can perform right action, but if we do not understand why we are performing that action, our action might be of no avail. In the next verse the Gita says:

Action is far inferior
to the yoga of insight, Arjuna.
Pitiful are those who, acting,
are attached to their action's fruits.

Understanding this truth brings us freedom. Attachment to outcomes limits us to the outcome we have defined as acceptable. Any outcome beyond what we have determined to be the only acceptable one leaves us unhappy, disappointed, and unable to experience spiritual growth from the situation.

Because our attachments are ego-based, the fruits of our actions are also ego-based. Look what I did! I acted and this wonderful result happened! Then, instead of acting simply for the sake of action, we act for the ego high that we get from the results of our actions.

Nonattachment is particularly difficult in relationships. We become attached to a person because that person feeds our ego. I've had people say to me, "But you must become attached to your spouse, children, and parents, because they are the ones you love most." It's difficult to understand loving someone dearly and yet being nonattached to them—giving them freedom to be their own person and live their lives as their karma dictates. Attachment is ego. Nonattachment is love.

Attachment creates a lot of drama because of its egoic nature. Nonattachment removes the drama from events by taking the emotional significance out of them. Attachment causes us to pour emotional energy into things. It lowers our pitch, reducing the energy we need to grow spiritually. Nonattachment helps us to neutralize our reactions to these things or events;

the drama becomes less exciting, so we are more positive. Our emotional appetite changes, and we have less desire for all this drama. We develop a sense of ease that helps us take the edges off life and move more easily through it.

In many cases, when people fall in love, it is not actually love, because it is based on the desire for the ego's happiness. We value the other person because they make us feel good, or because we believe they love us, which means we are lovable. Romantic relationships generally involve the senses—touching, kissing, hugging, having sex—all of which strengthen the attachment, enabling the ego to tighten its grip on the person we say we love.

This is why we suffer so deeply with the loss of someone we love. We feel it so deeply because of our attachment to the person and the feelings we have about the person. Death causes us to experience deep sorrow because we are now denied the feelings that gave us so much pleasure and satisfaction.

Pure love—unconditional love or *agape* (Greek for a godlike love)—is unmixed with attachment and stems entirely from a concern for others' happiness. This pure love, or unconditional love, which is really a true compassion, results in peace and happiness for both us and others. This makes the relationship flow naturally, peacefully, and without strain or effort. Whenever I hear people say that relationships have to be worked at in order to be successful, it reminds me of something that came to me shortly after my third marriage dissolved, even though after I'd spent so much time, energy, and effort trying to *make it work*: I have to work at my work; if I have to work at my relationship, maybe there is something wrong with it. If it cannot flow naturally and comfortably out of who we are as people, perhaps there is too much ego and attachment—too much "me" and not enough "us"—in the relationship. We should learn to distinguish between ego attachment and pure love, which wants the other to be happy. When two people are attached egotistically in a relationship that focuses solely on each individual, the love is not pure and unconditional. The relationship cannot survive unless it transcends attachment.

When we love without attachment, we truly love. We can then give our loved ones the space to be who they are and walk the path they are meant to walk. We can even allow them to die at their appointed time without inserting our own wants and needs into the picture.

9

LEARNING TO EMBRACE WHAT IS

In the twenty-first century we die in the embrace of hope. It burns like a perpetual fire; we expect that somehow it will save us, heal us, and bring us back into a life that we desire, not the fearsome slipping and sliding into darkness that only holds the promise of light. Hope, not religion, is the opiate of human beings. In the face of terminal illness, this hope takes the form of pills, surgery, chemotherapy, and other manmade cures that often do not work very well and only cause more suffering. Hope stands just out of reach, yet we keep grasping at it, clinging to life even if that life is filled with pain, agony, and sorrow so deep that it pulls us into the pits of hell. With every pill, every surgery, and every round of chemo, we believe we finally have reached the end of our pain and sorrow. But not yet! The pain continues, and people endure it because hope hangs bright and shining as the evening star, just out of reach. We grasp for it and watch it fade.

Hope arises from the Judeo-Christian worldview. The apostle Paul says that faith, hope, and love are the three major attributes of the Christian, and he adds that the greatest of these is love. Where does that leave faith and hope? When we become ill, many people say that having enough faith will bring healing. But is healing always about getting well? Can people be healed and yet remain in their illness? Of course!

Hope is future thinking. It is a form of wishful thinking that takes us beyond the *now* into some undefined place in the future, where we *hope* things will somehow be better than they are today. Hope feeds our suffering when we want things to be different. Hope is ambiguous. We hope for the best. We hope for health and healing. "I hope that everything is okay," we might say, when in actuality we need to shorten that sentence to "Everything is."

I have a friend who is very tuned into the spiritual. Whenever I ask her, "How are you?" she replies, "I am." I think that just about says it all. She *is*. No judgment about whether or not she is good or bad. She just *is*. Many times, particularly since Brent's death, people have asked, "How are you?" and I've replied, "I'm doing well," when I really am not. I'd like to scream, "I'm terrible! I feel sad! I'm feeling lonely!" But I don't want to burden people with my feelings of sadness or loneliness, so I just reply, "I'm fine." In reality, like all of the rest of us, I *am*.

Hope, as Pema Chödrön writes, is something to hold on to. It's the offering of theism. "Theism," she writes, "is a deep-seated conviction that there's some hand to hold: if we just do the right things, someone will appreciate us and take care of us. It means thinking that there's always a babysitter available when we need one." Hopelessness, on the other hand, "means that we no longer have the spirit for holding our trip together." The problem with hope is that it is trying to get ground under ourselves, trying to make ourselves and our lives solid, permanent, unchanging. Chödrön continues: "Believing in a solid, separate self, continuing to seek pleasure and avoid pain, thinking that someone 'out there' is to blame for our pain—one has to get totally fed up with these ways of thinking. One has to give up hope that this way of thinking will bring us satisfaction. Suffering begins to dissolve when we can question the belief or the hope that there's anywhere to hide."

Hopelessness is the place where there is no ground. "At every turn we realize once again that it's completely hopeless—we can't get any ground under our feet," Chödrön writes. "Nontheism is finally realizing that there's no babysitter that you can count on."

Believing in an anthropomorphic God who is supposed to be your babysitter becomes difficult, particularly when the babysitter leaves. Where was God during the Holocaust? many people ask. Where was God when my child was killed by a drunk driver? Was the babysitter on a break at that moment? Did the babysitter turn his back at the time and fail to see what was happening? Those are real issues for monotheists, who believe in a God that is supposed to be watching out for us, watching over us, and protecting us from the harmful things in this world.

There is harm in the hope of monotheism's anthropomorphic God. It leads us astray and sets us up for disappointment and disillusionment. Take the story of a lady named Jeanne. I encountered Jeanne on a Friday in 2005, in the gift shop of a resort hotel in Lake Geneva, Wisconsin, where she worked as a clerk. A friend and I were paying for some items when we noticed the magnetic bracelets hanging on a rack at the point of purchase. I commented that I often used magnetic therapy for aches and pains associated with my thumbs (probably caused from too many years of typing) and my knees. Not only did Jeanne have carpal tunnel syndrome in her hands, but she was also wearing a neck brace.

"I wished magnets would help me," she sighed. "I have to have neck surgery tomorrow."

"What happened to you?" I inquired.

She told how she had broken her neck while trying to force a shovel into some very hard ground in a cemetery. She had been planting flowers on the grave of her grandson, who was killed in a car wreck the day before his twenty-first birthday. His birthday was also Jeanne's birthday, and she was devastated by the event. Tearfully, she told us how the two of them had been especially close, especially because he lived with her for a number of years.

She pulled aside her sweater lapel to reveal a large button with a photo of her grandson on it, a happy-looking young man with dark hair and dark eyes, bright and filled with the confidence of youth.

If only the ground had been wetter, but the drought in the Midwest that summer had made the ground impossibly hard. She tried jumping up and down on the shovel to force the blade into the ground, but the shovel slipped, and she fell over backwards, hitting her head on the hard ground, breaking her neck and three ribs. "He was my favorite grandchild out of seventeen grandchildren. My daughter is devastated too. I don't know why God is doing this to me!" she exclaimed, the anger clearly rising up in her voice.

There was a drought in Jeanne's spirit as well. She was frightened and angry. She knew that she could no longer depend on the God she was taught to depend on in her Catholic faith. I felt a pang in my heart. I wanted to say something, anything, to help her.

"So that's my whole sad story," she concluded bluntly, tears welling in her eyes. She was so overwrought by the events of her life, so deeply saddened and hurt emotionally, and now physically with her injury, that it was all just too much for her.

"I can tell you," she continued in an emphatic voice, "if I don't live through this surgery, I'm ready to go and be with my grandson." She kept muttering about not understanding why God was doing this to her as she wrapped our purchases and placed them in bags.

Now I felt angry. Jeanne's Catholic religion and her belief in an anthropomorphic God had failed her. She could see no good in all of this, even after I encouraged to seek the lessons and ask God, "What am I supposed to learn?" She was too angry at God to see any good in her situation at all.

Her question, "Why is God doing this to me?" rang in my head the remainder of the day.

The problem of believing in an anthropomorphic God looms large when it comes to issues of illness, accident, and death—as much so today as in Job's day. Every time I get an email from a friend with regard to the blessings of God for all the good things we have, then I always must ask, "Who gives us the bad things in our lives?" If we are blessed because we are good and do all the "right" things—go to church, pray, pay tithes, and carry out other religious duties—why does God permit bad things to happen to these good people like Jeanne?

The only answer, of course, is karma. We all get the life we deserve, the life we have carved out for ourselves through our many past lives and the karma we create in each of our lifetimes. There is no anthropomorphic God, a God with the human qualities of cursing and blessing people and disliking some while loving others. Some might say that there is a Satan that gives curses and might even point to the Old Testament myth of Job, whom God and Satan used as the pawn in their game. This myth negates the idea of theodicy—God granting good for good and evil for evil. Bad things do happen to good people, not because they did anything to deserve it, as Job's friends found out, but because our life reflects all the karmic events that have ripened as our experiences. We all get the life we have created and earned for ourselves though karma. Simply put, we reap what we sow; the universal law of cause and effect is ever present, and even an anthropomorphic God cannot interfere with that. God cannot, by his own universal laws and principles, interfere with our karma. Otherwise, one must say that God is either all-powerful, but chooses to do nothing to save people from disaster or is not as powerful as people believe he is and simply *can't* do anything.

A Buddhist verse warns: "Do not lose yourself in the future." We can waste a lot of time hoping for something better, for a longer or healthier life. While hope can seem to promise some people that their future may be better, it is often a waste of mental energy. We find that in hoping, we spend too much time in the future and not enough embracing the now and learning not to suffer.

None of us really know how or when our karma will ripen or how it will play out in each lifetime.

Too often we allow life to just happen to us. The bumper sticker "Shit happens" pretty much defines the way we look at things. We allow stuff to happen, then blame someone else or something outside ourselves and fall into a funk. We must always remember that what happens isn't really happening *to* us but *because of* us. Ultimately, it's the result of choices we've made, the thoughts we've put into the universe, and the focus we've given to things.

Yet most people do not like this line of thinking; they do not want to believe they are responsible for the things that happen. Many adamantly refuse to believe that events in our lives are the result of our choices—either in this life or a previous life—and what we subsequently did with those.

Many years ago, Rabbi Harold Kushner wrote a book entitled *Why Bad Things Happen to Good People.* This question is one of the biggest dilemmas in human life. As Richard Smoley, one of my teachers in Theosophy, said once: "People always question why there is evil, but they never question why good things happen. That's because we expect the universe to be good, just, and fair on some level."

As Lama Surya Das has pointed out, we do not choose pain, but we do choose suffering. Why do we do this when the alternative is to embrace all that happens to us, ask the universe, "What is the lesson?" and move on? I do not know the answer to that. Perhaps it is a part of being human. It is being unable to see the big picture from this limited vantage point.

Living in opposition to our environment, in opposition to *what is*—that is what causes us stress. We are connected to the entire universe and all beings in it. When we live in opposition to what is, we get off balance, and that creates stress and illness. Living in opposition means fighting those things that come into our lives rather than embracing them, which brings on greater suffering.

Part 2

ILLNESS,
OLD AGE,
AND DEATH

10

IMMORTALITY: THE SEARCH
FOR THE FOUNTAIN OF YOUTH

Exactly how long *should* we live? The report *Mortality in the United States*, 2017, released by the US Department of Health and Human Services and National Center for Health Statistics in November 2018, revealed that during 2017, life expectancy at birth was 78.6 years for the total US population, a decrease from 78.7 years in 2016. This drop in life expectancy was blamed in part by an increase in suicide, from 13.5 per 100,000 in 2016 to 14.0 per 100,000 in 2017.

However, according to more recent numbers from the Centers for Disease Control and Prevention, the life expectancy for the US total population fell from 78.8 in 2019 to 77.8 years in the first half of 2020, a decline of 1.2 years. Deaths from Covid-19 contributed to the decline, as well as "deaths of despair," such as the rise in drug overdose deaths (93,000, up nearly 30 percent in 2020, according to provision statistics from the CDC). Death by suicide (which I discuss in a later chapter) also rose in 2017 by 3.7 percent, a continuing increase since 1999, according to the CDC report. These decreasing life-expectancy numbers are discouraging for those who believe a continued increase in life expectancy should be the norm as better health care and medical treatments create longevity. According the 2017 NCHS report, seven out of the ten leading causes of death (heart disease, cancer, unintentional injuries, chronic lower respiratory diseases, stroke, Alzheimer disease, diabetes, influenza and pneumonia, kidney disease, and suicide) decreased for one leading cause: cancer, which saw a 2.1 percent decrease.

We know that death is certain. No matter how many new medical treatments science develops or how many vitamins we take, the length of our lives cannot be determined by those factors alone. Expectations as to how long we *should* live—or *could* live if we do all the right things—are often disappointing to those who want increasing life expectancy.

"These sobering statistics are a wakeup call that we are losing too many Americans, too early and too often, to conditions that are preventable," said CDC director Robert Redfield in the article. Much of the reduction in our overall longevity has been driven by what sociologists call "despair" deaths. Drug-overdose deaths rose dramatically between 2015 and 2017, "particularly for adults between ages 25 and 54, with opioids being the primary culprit, "the article continued. Suicides (which I will discuss in a later chapter) rose 3.7 percent in 2017, "accelerating an increase in rates since 1999," the CDC reported. "This is extremely discouraging," said Christine Moutier, chief medical officer of the American Foundation for Suicide Prevention.

These disheartening statistics would appear to be due to events that are difficult to prevent. But why are scientists and doctors so concerned with how long people live? Can we live longer than the one hundred years that many people are experiencing in today's world? What can we do to extend our life, if anything? And would a longer life bring us greater happiness and satisfaction? Would it entail a healthy, vibrant lifestyle, or would we just spend more years in assisted living facilities or nursing homes?

The big question is why science is so eager to find a way to extend our human lifespan when, unfortunately, the emphasis has shifted from the quality of life to the *quantity* of life. The answer, of course, is the fear of death and the dying process and the uncertainty of what lies beyond. These fears—particularly of the dying process—drive our search for immortality, for the Fountain of Youth that has been said to exist throughout the ages. It strikes me as odd, but surveys consistently show that most people would like to live forever in these mortal bodies. In other words, they would like immortality.

Is immortality achievable? It is—and in fact is a reality—but not in these mortal bodies. As entities, we consist of three components: physical bodies, spiritual bodies, and mind/soul bodies. We are immortal, but not in the way people would like to be immortal. Our immortality involves physical decay and death, which people today do not want to be part of the picture. They want immortal life as they know it right here and now.

Some want immortality so desperately that they are willing to pay $100,000 annually to have their body cryogenically frozen in liquid nitrogen at a facility in Scottsdale, Arizona, so that they can be thawed and resume their "normal" life when a cure for the disease from which they died has been discovered, or when old age is no longer an issue.(By the way, the laboratory removes the head from the body so that it will fit in the tank, with the head in a separate holding tank. This whole process sounds like quite a feat of medical science—or science fiction.)

Longevity has become a major focus for the healthcare system, to the point where a large percentage (80 percent was the last statistic I read) of our healthcare dollars are being spent on people in their eighties and nineties during the final two years of life. This attempt to keep them alive shows little regard for the quality of life.

Living in the now is crucial for living fully. We have no past. Our past continually unfolds into our present, and our present enfolds our future, leaving nothing but the now, which consists of all that was and all that will be—the enfolding and unfolding of life.

Who says that living to be sixty-one years old (Brent's age when he died) is a bad thing? Many people only live to be twenty; some only live to be ten or five years old. My great-nephew was born with a rare genetic defect that gives his body an inability to process protein. At one point his parents were told that it was doubtful that he would live much into his young childhood, but at age sixteen, he is still alive and enjoying life to the extent he can with his disability.

All life—no matter how long or how short—has meaning. Each of us brings meaning with us when we take rebirth, and each of us imparts meaning into this life. The life of a person who lives to be one hundred isn't more meaningful than that of a person who lives to be only five, yet when almost anyone dies, people mourn that it was not long enough. People lament that "she died too soon" or "he went before his time" (as if we can know when a person's "time" is).

Life in all its stages takes on new meaning as we grow physically, emotionally, mentally, and spiritually through its stages. When we are sixteen, life means something entirely different than when we reach forty. By the time we reach our seventies or eighties, it means something different still: our perspective changes.

My mother received a letter from my family's attorney shortly after my father was killed in a car crash. A teenage driver had lost control on a wet road and hit my parents head-on (my mother was unhurt). The attorney told my mother he was sorry to hear of the "untimely death" of her husband, and he wanted to sue the family of the teenaged driver. I happened to be with my mother when that letter arrived, and my first comment to her was, "How does this attorney know that Daddy's death was untimely? Maybe it was the perfect time for him to die and the perfect means!"

My father had been diagnosed with a form of progressive muscular dystrophy when he was thirty-six years old. As he aged, it became progressively worse. When he reached his eighties, he rode on a motorized scooter and needed lifts, ramps, and a handicapped-accessible van to travel. When he reached the age of eighty-two, his activities were very limited. He had created a manufacturing company after taking early retirement from a large corporation and still ran the business with the help of my brothers. But he knew that his life could be one of being able to do nothing but lie in bed helpless, something he was not looking forward to. His one wish, as he often expressed it to me, was to die before my mother, because she was his perfect caregiver. On that day in January 2002, on a rain-slick road, Daddy got his wish. How perfect was that?

The Judeo-Christian tradition contributes much to this attitude of fear of death and its obsession with longevity with its teaching that we have one life only—this one only—in which to accomplish all we need to do. Even the movie actress Sally Field promotes the osteoporosis drug Boniva by telling the audience, "I've got this one life!" Some may find it comforting to believe that we come here only once—few want to chance coming back again into undesirable circumstances. Others find the idea of returning and resuming one's mission a pleasant thought.

Let's look at all this from another perspective. It seems that the people who want this life to be immortal are those who enjoy a good life, have a nice home with two cars, take vacations to the Caribbean every winter, and love their jobs, at which they make a lot of money. However, would this scenario never change?

Would people who live in Third World countries, suffer starvation, disease, and civil wars, and have never had jobs or money want immortality? I venture to say that these people would not want to be immortal. It's one thing to sit comfortably here in a First World country and wish for immortality, but it is quite another thing to wish for it in the depths of poverty, disease, and despair. In that situation, we'd probably wish for a quick end. Even reincarnation would not seem a good thing unless someone could be assured of being born in the United States or some other well-off nation.

But why do we seem to be suffering from so much disease,

even in the United States, where we have enough to eat and access to good medical care? Cancer seems to run rampant, although it is not as prevalent as heart disease. In the face of all the diseases we face, what chance for immortality do we have?

Looking at the evolution of the human being from an esoteric standpoint, one sees several important factors. Perhaps it is that over the past few hundred years, we have become denser in our physical form. This density creates opportunity for illnesses such as cancer, which involves cells that have lost their off switch and replicate uncontrollably. Is there a way, perhaps through meditation or other forms of mind work, of lightening our cells so that we can become more translucent, or perhaps transparent, once again? At that point, perhaps our bodies will conceivably be less prone to disease because they will have become lighter in density.

Eckhart Tolle says that awareness of the inner body slows down the aging process:

> As soon as your habitual state changes from being out of the body and trapped in your mind to being in the body and present in the Now, your physical body will feel lighter, clearer, more alive. As there is more consciousness in the body, its molecular structure actually becomes less dense. More consciousness means a lessening of the illusion of materiality.

Tolle is probably saying that we can revert to being more translucent or even transparent, like our early human progenitors, if we simply recognize that we are not our bodies. Nonetheless, we have bodies for a purpose, and there are functions that we can only carry out in our bodies, which is why we need them periodically in our various lifetimes.

Jeanne de Salzmann, a teacher of the Gurdjieff Work, told her student Ravi Ravindra, "The body is not only yours." Our individual bodies serve the collective body and contribute to it. Or as Madame de Salzmann says, "Clearly [the body] must serve something higher, otherwise it has no meaning."

The body exists for a higher purpose: to help the soul (atman) function on this lower level of consciousness. The body is the carrier of the higher Self. At the same time, the body likes to believe it is the all-important entity—the true self—and as a result ego takes over. The body consists of collapsed waves in the fabric of the universe, brought into our consciousness as particles and constructed by the mind as a house (but never a home) for the body. It is needed for this brief time span on this level of consciousness, but it changes, and what changes is impermanent.

Even so, giving up the body is difficult for most people, particularly in the West. We so strongly identify with our bodies that we fail to understand that there is neither a self-existent body that is inherently real nor even a self to inhabit this body. We finally reach a point where our body betrays us, grows old and sick, and is unable to support our souls and minds. It gives up the vital energy and exits its shell. Yet the ego clings to the body as a means of keeping the self intact, often refusing to let go of this shell or sheath, in which it feels its self-existence.

"You realize that death is an illusion, just as your identification with form was an illusion," Tolle tells us. "The end of illusion—that's all that death is. It is painful only as long as you cling to illusion." And I might add it is painful only as long as you cling to the mental construct of an inherently existent self.

Along those same lines, Mary Baker Eddy, founder of Christian Science, writes in her book *Science and Health with Key to the Scriptures*, first published in 1875, that failure to focus on the truth behind illusion is one of the causes of sickness. She taught that the "recuperative action of the system, when mentally sustained by Truth, goes on naturally" and that sickness is the "reverse of harmony." She also taught that to overcome sickness, the "mask" or the illusion of sin and sickness must be removed—"point out the illusion, and thus get the victory over sin and so prove its unreality." In other words, if we focus on the now and on the spiritual body and recognize the truth of our being, we cannot be fooled by the twin illusions of sickness and sin. As we meditate and come to understand the true nature of Mind, the cells become less dense and thus less subject to disease.

From ancient times on, it was believed that sin was the cause of illness. Today we may not acknowledge sin as the cause of illness, but we read in many books and magazines how the mental body and emotional body affect the physical body. One study found that people who are angry tend to get brain cancer more often than those who are at peace with themselves and their fellow beings. Whether or not that is merely a statistical fluke or a reality, I cannot say. But having been around angry people from time to time in my life, I can see where the emotions rise up into the head area as these people scream and yell at those to whom they are directing anger. The face gets contorted and red, and the words of hatred and anger echo throughout the person's head.

Mary Baker Eddy also taught that fear increases the incidence of disease: "You must not tell the patient that he is sick nor give names to diseases, for such a course increases fear, the foundation of disease, and presses more deeply the wrong mind-picture. A Christian Scientist's medicine is Mind, the divine Truth that makes man free."

This would fit quite well with the mind-body connection that many in the medical community are currently investigating. Mrs. Eddy might ask them, "What took you so long?" The Old Testament says, "As a man thinks, so is he" (Proverbs 23:7). Quantum physicists tell us that we each create our own reality. The mind directs the body.

Mrs. Eddy writes:

> We shall never affirm concerning the body what we do not wish to have manifested. We shall not call the body weak, if we would have it strong; for the belief in feebleness must obtain in the human mind before it can be made to manifest on the body, and the destruction of the belief will be the removal of its effects. Science includes no rule of discord but governs harmoniously. "The wish," says the poet, "is ever father to the thought."

In other words, do not call out the illness unless you wish it to be manifested in you. We know people get sick and die, but people who refuse to acknowledge their illness or any obstruction to their health retain their idea of health; thus, they retain their health in spite of it all. It was amazing to me that throughout Brent's eighteen months with esophageal cancer, he never thought of himself as sick or as having cancer. Instead, he went back to work as a sales manager, dealt with his clients in his usual jovial manner, and never mentioned the cancer. He loved driving his Corvette, and we engaged in the activities of the Corvette Club to which we belonged. In fact, four months before he died, he bought a new 'Vette because the new ones were easier to drive, and he had a wonderful time with it.

Mrs. Eddy believed that the mind governs the body and that giving into sickness, failing to resist the temptation to believe in it, is what makes us sick. She defined sickness as "error" and believed that the road to good health lies in "Truth." That is much like the Buddhist belief that if you know the true nature of mind, the truth about the nature of reality on this level of consciousness, you are free from the illusions that bind you to this consciousness.

The book *On Being Human: Where Ethics, Medicine, and Spirituality Converge*, by Daisaku Ikeda, a Buddhist monk and president of Soka Gakkai International; René Simard, a well-known authority on cancer research; and Guy Bourgeault, a professor at the University of Montreal, offers a diverse approach to disease and wellness and provides some vital insight into medical ethics and spirituality.

Ikeda proposes that sickness of the physical body is caused by the disharmony of the four elements that make up the physical body—earth, wind, fire, and water—and correspond to the flesh, breath, temperature, and liquids. Secondly, this disharmony is also caused by our inability to embrace change and adapt to various alterations in our external environment. We experience events that cause us fear and upset us mentally and emotionally, resulting in physical changes in the body's mechanisms.

Third, irregular meditation can also be a cause for disharmony and illness, as can any disruption of the rhythms in our daily life patterns.

The fourth cause, which may be the one least comprehensible to Westerners, is a demon. However, that "demon" can be "bacteria or viruses," which have certainly caused mental stress and upset during the past year of pandemic.

Fifth, illness can come from "malevolent forces." The chaotic instincts and desires in human nature unbalance the functions of the body and the mind. Buddhism teaches that mental illnesses arise mainly from delusions like wrath and greed.

Sixth, there is karma-caused illness, which is something that we Westerners generally do not like to acknowledge, primarily because we do not like to believe that we brought illness to ourselves. Those who practice the Eastern philosophies find karma and its connection to physical illnesses relatively easy to accept because the "powerful energy of karma" may be a force in our life energy, Ikeda explains. Karma from past lives may also affect our psychological (mental and emotional) energy. Any "distortions" in our karmic vital energy can cause illness.

Buddhism's focus on the teachings of death is key to learning how to live. "First learn about death, and then about other matters," Ikeda advises. As both statements suggest, learning about death enriches life. True health does not mean the absence of illness. Rather, it is a life-state characterized by an openness to the hearts and minds of others and to the environment. There is also a constant readiness to exercise the creative ability to serve society. To maintain health in that sense until the last moment is to die with dignity.

Ikeda added that his mentor, Josei Toda, "radiated health in the true sense of the word, even after he became ill." (And I might add, so did Brent. It was the thing that people noticed most about him—that he radiated happiness and health until the day he died. He often commented, "I don't have cancer— the cancer has me.")

Bourgeault then commented that his mentor, Mr. Cormier, also maintained his health in the face of cancer, saying, "'I'm not sick. It is just my body that is being attacked by cancer.' He fulfilled the definition of health as something a person can deal with physically, psychologically, economically, socially, and culturally. He never regarded his cancer as a 'sickness' but as a condition he could continue to cope with in the above ways." By removing the "I" from the situation and not identifying with the disease or with his body, he was able to overcome the suffering that comes with illness. That is how Brent dealt with his cancer.

A few years ago, one of my best friends died. It was the end of a two-year journey in which she remained happy and joyful even though she was ill. A follower of the Science of Mind tradition, she believed that her thoughts were all-important to her well-being. She accepted medical help through her naturopath, who provided various remedies for her to take. At one point she went to a medical doctor, who told her that he suspected liver cancer. She rejected the diagnosis and declined a liver biopsy. She would not say the word *cancer* from that point on, believing that speaking the word gives energy to the disease. One day she wrote to me that she was feeling quite ill, and other friends had suggested that she go to the ER. "I do not want to do that. I don't want my life to become tests and treatments that will make my life worse." I replied that I supported her decision to live—and die—in the way she wanted. She thanked me for that support. A few months later, she died peacefully at home with a caregiver at her side.

Since my friend Diane's death in August 2019, I've thought a lot about our many conversations about Brent's illness and death, and how he died on his own terms. I'm sure that Diane had thoughts of those conversations as she lay dying in the way she wanted to go—peacefully releasing her mind to the all-pervading intelligence of the universe.

Curing chronic illnesses like cancer and diabetes, which seem to cut life short, is a stated goal of the medical community. But will better treatments really make extended life worth living, or will we just live longer in physical and mental misery? When we wish for a Fountain of Youth, do we know what we are really asking for? Many people who wish for very long lifespans are often young, healthy, and in the prime of their life and careers. I've never met anyone in their eighties and nineties who says to me, "I sure hope I can live another twenty or thirty years."

As my mother's best friend used to tell her, "We all have a shelf life!"

11

THE BUSINESS OF ILLNESS:
THE COST OF KEEPING US ALIVE

A lmost without discussion, the primary moral principle underlying medical practice became the obligation to prolong life regardless of the toll in suffering, poor quality of life, or cost.

—DIANE MEIER, quoted in *Knocking on Heaven's Door*,

by Katy Butler

Illness in the United States today is big business. Some call it the healthcare industry, but a more appropriate term—one I've seen used from time-to-time in editorials—is the "illness-care" industry. It is from illness, or the possibility of illness, that the industry reaps its huge and growing profits. People take pharmaceuticals seeking cures for ailments, pain, sickness, and other health threats because they fear death. They believe that if they can ward off death by taking a drug, they will be safe. Thus, it is in the interest of big business to sustain the illness culture by making pharmaceuticals a part of our everyday lives, which often allows health problems to take on a life of their own.

The idea of "fighting" to hang on to one's body—our most prized possession—is one primary reason people agree to take many of the drugs offered, even though they usually have side effects than can often make the condition worse in different ways.

As I have already observed, in the Western tradition, fighting is a good thing. In addition, many people would feel guilty if they were to give up and say that they would rather leave this physical existence. Many patients try to hang on for their families, who might feel slighted or unwanted or unloved if the patient decides to go quietly into that good night. Patients show that they are truly fighting to stay alive so that their families and friends won't feel rejected.

People, especially the elderly, take enormous amounts of drugs. Many doctors see being elderly as a disease that needs to be cured rather than a stage of life that we will reach if we live long enough. Over the years I've volunteered for organizations that assist the elderly with grocery shopping, friendly visiting, and other tasks. Many of these people take a dozen or more pills a day. Most can't even tell you what the pills are for. A doctor hands them a prescription; they fill it and take the pills.

Merck, the makers of Vioxx, the controversial painkiller that is believed to have contributed to the deaths of people who took it, is fighting thousands of lawsuits over the drug, which it pulled from the market. One woman, the widow of a man who took Vioxx and subsequently died of a heart attack, was interviewed by a reporter about her lawsuit. She said, "If we had known of the dangers of this drug, he would have never taken it."

I am not sure about that. The dangerous side effects of drugs are announced briefly on television commercials and published in several pages of fine-print advertisements in magazines, but somehow people tend to either miss those warnings or decide that it won't happen to them. They say yes to the drugs despite the warnings of dangerous side effects, even death. That's what the drug companies count on.

Now there is oxycodone (Oxycontin), an opioid that is the latest and greatest at treating pain. The extensive use of opioids has created an addiction crisis that is costing the U.S. millions of dollars in treatment and thousands of lives lost to this drug. In 2019, Purdue Pharma, the producer of Oxycontin, had more than 2,000 lawsuits pending against it filed by individuals and governments nationwide. "Prior to 1986, opioids were really used only to treat acute pain, cancer pain or terminally ill patients. The use of opioids to treat non-cancer pain, was controversial," said Denis G. Patterson, DO, in an article in the August 2017 issue of *Psychology Today*. Tests performed prior to 1986 with a median daily dose of less than twenty-milligram equivalents of morphine per day showed a lack of "clinically significant adverse events," leading doctors to believe that opioids were safe to use generally. In August 2019, Purdue Pharma offered $10 billion to 12 billion in a tentative settlement.

Because everyone wants to be happy and free from suffering, doctors hand out these dangerously addictive drugs like they are aspirin. According to medical reports, opioids account for a large number of deaths among the elderly. As our bodies age, we experience the disintegration of the body, and along with that comes the aches and pains of old age. The answer for many lies in dangerous opiates, which certainly alleviate pain but can also numb us to living, and even be the cause of the thing we fear most: death.

My mother, born in 1921, was very pill adverse. She questioned everything and primarily took only vitamins. Once, when she was eighty-two, a doctor prescribed an osteoporosis drug for her on the premise that since she was elderly, her bones must be thinning (the test showed "some loss of bone density"), so he wanted her to take a drug. Dutifully she took the prescription to the drugstore and had it filled. However, the nasal spray that was prescribed resulted in mother getting dead-jaw syndrome, resulting in the loss of her teeth.

Many women who have taken drugs for osteoporosis have experienced dead-jaw syndrome as well as thigh-bone fractures and breaks, as the drugs for osteoporosis turn the bones to stone instead of building calcium. Women who are said to have fallen and broken their femur have actually had their femurs break *before* they fell. Recently a friend of mine asked for prayer for an elderly friend who had "fallen and broken both her femurs." Given that the femur is the strongest bone in a human's body, it was very unlikely that she had fallen and broken both femurs. For this very reason, a class-action lawsuit is being pursued against this bone-density drug.

My mother began reading the fine print that came with drugs. She read the entire piece of paper (she said it was eighteen inches long and seven inches wide) accompanying one drug a doctor prescribed for her. The paper was filled with warnings of potential side effects. After reading this, she threw the pills away. No way was she going to take something for a perceived "problem" that is a natural result of aging, particularly a drug that could give her more problems—for which she would need more drugs. That is how elderly people get on this merry-go-round. They are given drugs to cure symptoms and side effects of side effects of other drugs, until they are taking massive amounts of pills that cost them thousands of dollars each month.

Promoting treatments that will ultimately have no effect but to prolong a person's misery is in the best interest of the medical industry. Follow the money, as they taught us in journalism school. What would happen to the billions of dollars spent on cancer treatment if everyone had the attitude that Brent had when he was diagnosed with esophageal cancer? He had the surgery but refused radiation and chemotherapy, and instead of living the six months that the oncologist said he would live without chemo and radiation, he lived for eighteen months, and worked and traveled, embracing his life, and finally dying peacefully at home under hospice care. If everyone understood that their path might just be to embrace the disease, go with the flow, live with an attitude of love and acceptance, and reject the treatments that doctors recommend when it is known that the treatments will not cure, only prolong misery, the medical industry would go bankrupt.

In the *Wall Street Journal* on October 21, 2003, Kevin Helliker wrote an essay about his own confrontation with mortality, "Denying Death No More." Diagnosed with an aortic aneurysm the previous year, Helliker was confronted with the possibility of sudden death. He talks about how the knowledge of one's health problems can prompt one to do things differently, sometimes for the worst. Focusing on one's illness can bring on the very thing that one is trying to avoid, a belief with which people who practice the Science of Mind tradition would agree. The mind is a powerful tool, and it creates our reality; our thoughts can attract or bring to us whatever we focus on. If we refuse to acknowledge the power of illness, the illness cannot hurt us. That is also true in an esoteric sense. Can anything really hurt the mind/soul? No. Disease and accidents can kill the body, but nothing can harm the mind/soul, which is the seat of our divine nature.

The fact that we can receive hundreds of tests to diagnose any and all illnesses is, in some ways, a blessing, but mostly a curse. Helliker points out that in theory, the knowledge that test results give us doesn't always help us come up with a solution. In fact, while ignorance may be bliss, then the knowledge of what is going on in our bodies often brings up fears and uncertainties that may increase our anxiety and make our situation worse. There are instances when doing nothing can be the best option, but in most cases, people want something to be done—anything—to fix the problem even though the "fix" also comes with risks and may not provide the optimum cure.

A good friend, Marian, lived with blocked carotid arteries—one 80 percent blocked, the other 60 percent blocked—for ten years after she was diagnosed at age fifty-six. She took blood thinners, kept on smoking and enjoying her wine. She didn't have insurance when diagnosed—she only worked part-time—so surgery was out of the question. Her doctor told her that surgery could kill her as much as the blocked arteries, so she went on, ignoring the arteries and enjoying life. Each year, when she'd return to the doctor for her checkup, he would say half-jokingly, "Are you still alive?" Marian, who had a great sense of humor, would laugh and joke about how nothing could kill her until she decided it could. She died peacefully in her sleep at age sixty-seven, the Saturday before Mother's Day, with plans for a family picnic with her youngest son and his wife the next day. Marian had a good life and a good death.

Helliker writes that "to live daily with the knowledge of death is not all bad." He notes that knowing about his aneurysm has altered the way he looks at life. "I'm now less bent on reaching old age than on enjoying my present age." Instead of being even more careful about his health, the knowledge has had "the opposite effect."

We should all learn to accept the fact of our own death and, like Helliker, learn "to live daily with the knowledge of death." Buddhism encourages us to meditate on our own death, in which we visualize the dying process, seeing how we die by gradually losing the vital energy, the life force, and moving gradually up our "central channel" through the *ushnisha* center at the crown of the head. We are encouraged to think about our own death daily so that if it should happen suddenly, we will not be caught unaware. Conscious awareness of our death on a daily basis helps us to appreciate life, be grateful for every day, and learn to live more fully in the now.

After writing about his condition, Helliker received a memorable email from an unsympathetic reader: "I have bad news for you and all the other health nuts. One of these days you are going to die." Yes! That's the point! We all need to learn to live life to the fullest, embracing the knowledge that we are going to die. It is a certainty. In fact, think of this: the leading cause of *death* is *birth*!

That stunning truth hits hard in a country whose populace believes that we can keep death at bay indefinitely, that if people take enough medications and the antiaging gurus can come up with enough new hormones, we can stave off old age and death. Perhaps it is because we have never learned how to die that so many of us in the United States do not know how to live. We chase after life to the point that the very thing we are running from catches up to us and surprises us. The "worried well" in this country take drugs and submit to tests for perceived diseases, only to be mown down by something they could have never imagined would happen to them.

As Shakespeare says in *Julius Caesar*, "A coward dies a thousand times before his death, but the valiant taste of death but once." Fear of death is perhaps the worst fear that we humans must face, but as Shakespeare continues: "It seems to me most strange that men should fear, seeing that death, a necessary end, will come when it will come." Helliker notes that diagnoses and tests come with options for living, no matter what the result. Oftentimes, people who get positive test results feel, as Helliker did, "betrayed"—that all of their efforts to eat right, exercise, and be healthy were for nothing. However, knowing that he had an aneurysm was also very freeing for Helliker. It gave him permission to live his life without the end goal of being "perfect" or even the expectation of living to be a hundred years old.

In a way, Helliker is relieved of the unknowing that surrounds his life and his death. Brent found himself in the same position. One day a coworker asked him how he could be so happy knowing that he was going to die. "We're all going to die," he replied. "I'm lucky because I know what I'll die of, and about when I'll die. That's a big mystery for most people."

To me, knowing that, ultimately, I will die doesn't lessen my responsibility for taking good care of myself. I try to do good things for my body, such as eating well and taking vitamins, but I don't deny myself a piece of chocolate and a glass of wine every day, or fried chicken, mashed potatoes, and gravy now and then. I eat what I feel like eating and sometimes even eat what I'm craving. I realize that while my body is a gift, ultimately it is a temporary container. Will I enjoy life any more or live a week longer if I don't eat a piece of tasty chocolate? Or put real butter on my toast each morning? Will I only live to be ninety-two instead of ninety-three? Will it matter? It's not so much how long we live, but how *well* we live. I try to show my appreciation for my body by taking as good a care of it as I can, but to deny myself some of the joys of this material level of consciousness would show no appreciation of what life is meant to be.

Writing in the November 17, 2003, issue of *Businessweek*, in an article titled "Getting Rational about Rationing," Catherine Arnst reported that "mean medical expenditures for senior citizens was $37,581 in the final year of life vs. $7,365 for other years" or 27 percent of Medicare's budget. An article in *Health Affairs* noted that in 2014, the mean per capita spending for individuals in the last twelve months of life was "reaching

$80,000 in the US." According to the study (*Medicare Cost at End of Life*, published in March 2019 in *The American Journal of Hospice & Palliative Care*), estimates of the percentage of Medicare costs in 2015 for patients in the last year of life ranged from 13 percent to 25 percent, depending on the type of care received. The largest portion of Medicare expenditures occur in the last six months of life, with an increasing number of Medicare patients choosing hospice. However, many hospice patients are living longer than six months (the estimated prognosis of time a person has remaining to qualify for hospice care).

Arnst, writing in 2003, said that the "mean medical expenditure for senior citizens was $37,581 in the final year of life, vs. $7,365 for other years. Medicare spends 27 percent of its budget on patients in the last year of life—and those funds serve only 5 percent of enrollees," all because we in this country have a horror of death. According to an article in *Health Affairs*, since then the figures have risen dramatically: in 2014, the mean per capita spending for individuals in the last twelve months of life was "reaching $80,000 in the U.S.; 44.2 percent of that was hospital spending. The final three months of life accounted for 57.6 percent of medical care spending in the U.S. Healthcare spending accounts for a much larger share of the GDP in the U.S. that any other developed country."

A 2013 *Forbes* blog by Michael Bell cited Dr. Susan Dale Block, chair and director of psychosocial oncology and palliative care at the Dana Farber Cancer Institute and Brigham & Women's Hospital, who found in a study "that the less money spent in this time period (the last year and month) the better the death experience is for the patient." The study concluded that "no matter how much money is spent during the last year and month, if the person is sick enough, the effort makes things worse . . . making the patient endure more bad experiences on a daily basis. The patient's quality of life is being sacrificed by increasing the cost of death."

The push by many in the medical community for life at all costs versus quality of life is detrimental to patients and does nothing to help dying persons have a good death. "You can only ensure quality of life by having a discussion early on about how they want to live their life to the end the best possible way," wrote Bell.

We view death as a terrible thing that we cannot allow to happen to anyone. How sad that even doctors cannot talk about death and dying to dying people and their families! It is almost as if it reflects a failure on their part. Dr. Tropper, a radiologist who treated Brent when he had cancer, was visibly relieved when we explained what we wanted for Brent. Knowing that his cancer was aggressive and that he would probably die within a year or less, we opted for minimal treatment to reduce the tumor without interfering with Brent's work schedule. Dr. Tropper commented that he rarely saw patients that were even willing to admit death as a possibility, much less a probability; our attitude was a refreshing change from the norm.

The nearly bankrupt state of our healthcare system in the United States may force our hand in learning how to understand life and death. With many hospitals already rationing treatments and medication because of cost, can we afford to use every measure to keep people alive just because we can, or because we as a society do not understand death or life?

Perhaps when the healthcare system goes bankrupt, forcing us to look at rationing even more seriously, we will have progressed enough spiritually to understand that death is a natural event and is part of life. To allow the very aged and the very sick the privilege of dying with dignity—even to the point of teaching rituals for helping them make the transition into the astral plane—will be a huge step in the spiritual healing of this country. As long as we grasp after life, grasp after our bodies, and refuse to learn nonattachment, we will be spiritually stunted.

12

THE BUSINESS OF ILLNESS: PROSPERING FROM THE FEAR OF DEATH

If you've ever wondered who benefits most from our fear of death, take a look at the big pharmaceutical companies, whose business it is to create drugs that promise to cure what ails us, or at least to make our chronic illnesses manageable. (I doubt the goal is to actually *cure* any of the major chronic diseases such as cancer or diabetes—that would be killing the goose that lays the golden eggs.) Many oncology drugs are created to extend the life of patients with cancer—sometimes for several years—but while the quantity of one's days may be increased, the quality of one's life may be extremely compromised. Why people agree to taking devastating drugs to prolong life and suffer the accompanying misery varies from person to person.

Death comes when our karma for our death ripens, which is why we cannot predict our death or what we die of or how we will die. In spite of taking a statin drug, Tim Russert, the TV news reporter and moderator on the popular political news show *Meet the Press*, died of a massive heart attack in his office while preparing for the next Sunday's television show, at the relatively young age of fifty-three. We learn that we can't predict these things. When our number is up, it's up. When our karma for our death ripens, it ripens.

In between birth and death, there is this thing called life, and much of our life in these modern times is spent focusing on our health. Being healthy typically means being free of disease or physical impairment. The health industry is almost as big as the illness industry, as more of us focus on our bodies in our desire to be healthy. We want to be slim, trim, fit, and free of illness. To achieve that, there are thousands of vitamins and health foods that promise the optimum in nutrition and eating; diet programs, pills, and surgeries to reduce weight and remove fat; gyms on every corner for a daily workout; and medical tests that can examine every cell of our bodies for some illness that might sneak up on us unawares.

Many younger people depend on a fitness regimen and vitamins, as well as on other "natural" types of treatments, to keep themselves healthy. All of that is good! Taking care of the body we're given for this lifetime is a good thing and offers the rewards of keeping us free from illness, at least to a certain extent. Yet no matter how many miles we run a day or how many vitamins we take, we are going to live until we die. It's as simple as that.

My family, on both of my parents' sides, has a history of being very healthy and very long-lived. But disease happens. Rheumatic fever meant my father's mother had a bad heart, and she died in 1945, at age forty-four. My dad's father was from a family of seven children who all lived to ripe old ages and died of natural causes, and it was a pleasure to know all my great-aunts and great-uncles. My grandfather, however, who was the picture of health at age seventy-nine, was killed on December 24, 1975, in an automobile wreck while driving to buy Christmas presents. My dad was killed on that same road in February 2002, at the of age eighty-two. Death comes at seemingly strange times and places. No matter how hard we've worked at staying healthy, when our time has come, death takes us. Even modern medicine can't save us from this ultimate fate.

"Americans are hooked on a powerful illusion—that modern medicine, self-discipline and denial can together forestall death," writes Ann Toews in the *Wall Street Journal*. Toews gives us some interesting insights into two authors' experiences of mortality. One, Kate Bowler (*Everything Happens for a Reason, and Other Lies I've Loved*), is a thirty-seven-year-old mother and divinity-school professor who wrote her book while experiencing stage 4 colon cancer. Bowler's belief in theodicy—that God gives health and wealth to those who follow his commandments—has let her down. Her previous book, published in 2013, was a history of the prosperity gospel in America. In her case, this gospel failed.

Barbara Ehrenreich is an atheist, Toews tells us, "who takes comfort in the idea of an 'animate universe' of life and possibility." The seventy-six-year-old author of *Natural Causes: An Epidemic of Wellness, the Certainty of Dying, and Killing Ourselves to Live Longer*, Ehrenreich "goes after the same cultural illusion of mastery" of cancer. "Expressing her disappointment that the "immune cells and antibodies" designed to keep us safe from invaders such as cancer actually "aid and abet the proliferation of disease, she feels nothing short of betrayal," writes Toews. Ehrenreich conducted her doctoral research in the late 1960s on "macrophages, immune cells widely accepted as 'good guys' in the fight against harmful elements in the body," so she knows whereof she speaks in this regard.

Both women, Toews points out, have "chosen to forgo extreme medical intervention and to face the inevitable."

That is what Brent chose as well, which is probably what helped him live about a year longer than most people with esophageal cancer. Certainly, that is not a path that doctors approve of, but then they make their living selling chemo and radiation. It is rather ironic that Brent's sister, Nadine, died just before Thanksgiving in 2019, from the side effects of her first round of chemotherapy. And that Brent and Nadine's father died of stomach cancer while being treated with chemotherapy, which led him to be horribly sick, as Brent told me. Nadine, who was thirteen at the time of their father's death, had been afraid of their father's illness, a fear that she carried with her throughout her life. The cancerous polyp (which had been found during a routine colonoscopy) and surrounding tissue that had been removed from her colon made her prognosis "good," according to one of her daughters. But they recommended a three-month regimen of chemo just to be "safe." She died at home during the night after her first treatment at age seventy-four.

Ehrenreich "finds reasons to doubt our faith in Western 'rituals' of medical examinations, expensive wellness regimens and a glut of evidence-poor tests bemoaning precious time spent trying, uselessly, to prevent all manner of ailment," Toews tells us. She quotes from Ehrenreich's book: "'Conflict may be endemic to the human world, with all its jagged inequities, but it must be abolished in the individual,' she wryly concludes of the wellness movement. 'To what end? To feel good, of course, which is the same as feeling powerful.'"

Disease, both its diagnosis and treatment, is big business. Take cancer, for example. Who can possibly know how many dollars are being spent finding a cure for this devastating disease? Yet for all the dollars spent each year in research—new drugs, new treatments, new diagnostic tools, and other forms of care—people continue to die at about the same rate from cancer as they did thirty years ago. There is unlikely to be a cure for it, because despite the rhetoric we hear about it, a cure would devastate the billion-dollar cancer industry.

No wonder it angers oncologists when their patients reject chemotherapy. A friend whose mother died of pancreatic cancer refused treatment. The oncologist got angry, telling her, "You'll die in two months if you don't have chemo." My friend's mother replied, "Well, if I have chemo, I'll die in six months, and it will be a miserable six months." She chose instead to treat herself with alternative therapies, vitamins, and spiritual methods and lived another eighteen months after her diagnosis.

Cancer is perhaps the biggest illness industry in the United States. Large, extravagantly built centers such as MD Anderson Cancer Center and Cancer Treatment Centers of America, along with local and regional cancer centers, dot the landscape in this country. They all tout their ability to cure cancer with their specialty treatments. However, a 2018 article by Steve Salerno in the *Wall Street Journal* criticized the many TV advertisements promoting these centers because cancer treatment or "Cancer, Inc.," as Salerno calls it, has become extremely competitive. By 2020, Salerno writes, Cancer, Inc. is projected to be vying for some $207 billion in billings. "It is less a war on cancer than a war on truth and on vulnerable consumers," he contends.

As Salerno notes, while TV ads depict beautiful scenes of people who go to these centers to be cured using breakthrough technology, few provide the real numbers of five-year survival rates: cervical cancer, 69 percent; leukemia, 63 percent; ovarian cancer, 46 percent; cancer of the brain and nervous system, 35 percent; lung cancer, 19 percent; liver cancer, 18 percent; and pancreatic cancer, 9 percent, according to the American Cancer Society. Salerno wonders how these numbers justify the exorbitant costs of these centers, which take only cash or private health insurance (no Medicare or Medicaid patients allowed), which means if you are wealthy, you can get these treatments if you so choose.

These cancer centers, oncologists, and drug companies prey on people who are fearful of losing their life to the disease. They offer hope in the form of abject suffering through these treatments, yet those who survive the treatments might live only a few years—or a few months—longer. Hope is an illusion of life. The fear of death impels people ill with cancer to consent to any and all treatments and spend their life's savings or more in an attempt to be cured.

However, cancer is the ideal shapeshifter. It will mutate into any form to perpetuate itself into almost every part of the body. If anyone is "cured," it is less an actual cure than a true miracle.

Perhaps some people can use their minds to chase this shape-shifter from their bodies. We just don't know. The path is different for each of us and, again, none of us knows the day of our death or the outcome of our treatment. Some will live, some will die sooner.

A person who was promoting natural cures claimed to have a memo from a major drug manufacturer saying that the company's intent was to make cancer "a manageable chronic illness." According to this person, this means the drug company can keep making more drugs that will manage the symptoms of the illness but offer no cure. A cure, after all, would put these companies out of business. But if cancer is a manageable chronic disease, drugs will continue to be needed over the long term.

People wear T-shirts or buttons that say "I'm a cancer survivor"—thus giving life and an identity to this disease. Many who have been cured of cancer continue to identify with the disease by *declaring themselves* to be cancer survivors. They affiliate with other survivors in 10K runs and 5K walks to raise more money to find the cure. They continue to use and identify with the name "cancer" and to make it part of who they are, which continues to give the disease power over them. That becomes their identity, their label. They wear it like a badge.

If the drug companies truly found a cure—the magic bullet for out-of-control replicating cells—does anyone really believe that they would release it to the market? It would be the end of the entire culture that we have built up around this disease. It would also mean the end of huge empires that have been erected around cancer, such as research institutes, hospitals, and drug companies.

Keeping the cancer alive and thriving appears to be the goal of healthcare workers, drug makers, and even patients and survivors themselves. To keep the disease at the forefront and give it life, we have taught people to identify with it, to make it a part of who they are so that the cancer can continue to thrive.

In *The Power of Now*, Eckhart Tolle talks about surrender as a means of overcoming life situations. "Surrender is inner acceptance of what is without any reservations," he writes. "We are talking about your life—this instant—not the conditions or circumstances of your life, not what I call your life situation."

Our life situations happen to us in time, but we exist as spiritual beings in what Tolle calls the "timeless Now." In that state there are no problems; thus, he says, "there is no illness either." That may sound simplistic, but anyone who studies or practices Eastern religions, particularly Buddhism, understands this concept. All persons as teachers, all poison as medicine, say the Buddhists. Tolle continues:

> The belief in a label that someone attaches to your condition keeps the condition in place, empowers it, and makes a seemingly solid reality out of a temporary imbalance. It gives it not only reality and solidity but also a continuum in time that it did not have before. By focusing on this instead and refraining from labeling it mentally, illness is reduced to one or several of these factors: physical pain, weakness, discomfort, or disability. That is what you surrender to—now. You do not surrender to the ideal of "illness."
>
> Withdraw from the illness. Do not give it a past or

future. Let it force you into intense present-moment awareness—and see what happens.

Tolle adds that if anyone reading his book is ill and gets angry
at what he says, it "is a clear sign that the illness has become part
of your sense of self and that you are now protecting your identity—as well as protecting the illness. The condition labeled
'illness' has nothing to do with who you truly are."

How true! Brent was invited to attend cancer support
groups. He refused to go, saying that he did not want to associate with people who were that involved in their illness. He preferred to go on with his life as usual, be around healthy people,
and do the things he usually did. He did not want to buy into
the idea that he was a cancer patient.

In *Science and Health*, Mary Baker Eddy wrote that illness
is nonexistent unless we give it a name. When we do this, we
begin to identify with that illness, and it becomes who we are;
we give in to it. This gives it power not only over our physical
bodies but our mental and spiritual bodies as well. "You are not
sick until a doctor tells you that you are," she wrote. Could it
be that the moment we accept a doctor's diagnosis and agree
to take medicine, we are creating the illness in our minds? And
once we have agreed to the diagnosis and begun the "cure," we
have begun to identify with the illness as deeply as we do with
our bodies. To learn that "I am *not* my body" is one of the greatest of life's lessons.

For many people with cancer, treatments mostly delay the
inevitable. A business associate of mine who had become a good
friend was diagnosed with breast cancer. She had a lumpectomy,

with some lymph-node removal, then went through a round of radiation followed by a round of chemotherapy. The chemo did its usual damage, killing the nerves in her feet, which meant that she was in terrible pain and had trouble walking or standing. Three years later, she was diagnosed with a form of leukemia, often called "smoldering leukemia," as the bone marrow stops producing red blood cells. It too was a consequence of the chemotherapy.

After nearly a year of increasing weekly platelet transfusions, the doctors told her that there was nothing else to do except a bone-marrow transplant. However, at sixty-five, she was past the age at which they like to perform this treatment. She told me what the doctors told her. "They've given me a death sentence," she stated flatly.

"Well, Jeanette, the minute we take our first breath we're given a death sentence," I said. "We're all under a death sentence."

On October 2, 2007, Jeanette had a bone-marrow transplant. The pretreatment was horrendous: full-body radiation followed by huge doses of chemo drugs so that the new marrow would take. After three grueling weeks in the hospital, she went home. She had a feeding tube, because the chemo had ravaged her mouth and esophagus with canker sores. She had debilitating diarrhea and was losing weight. She suffered terribly for another seven weeks before she was liberated from this earthly level of pain and suffering.

None of us know how many days or weeks or months we have left. We hear of people who leave home to go to the store or to a friend's house for dinner and get broadsided by a red-light runner. That's it. Life's over for this round!

It's not important how we die. A business trip to Los Angeles turned tragic for a business acquaintance of mine who died in one of the planes that crashed into the World Trade Center, leaving behind a wife and two young sons. My father died in a car wreck; many members of my family, of extreme old age. It's just not important how we die! *What is important is how we live!* Do we take the time each day to be grateful for this life and make the most of it? To enjoy the way the sky looks? To feel joy when our children or grandchildren call to say hi? To help others who aren't as fortunate as we are? As my father used to say, "We tend to think we have it worse than anyone until we meet someone who's much worse off than we are." This was something he had to learn. His adult-onset muscular dystrophy kept him from doing many of the things he wanted to do, yet he found many other things to do, such as starting a successful business, investing in real estate, and, along with a builder friend, creating homes for people.

From the moment we are born, we are confronted with the specter of death. In fact, however, the physical life is the illusion, as is the belief that we are separate from Divine Mind and from everyone else. The soul-mind is the reality.

In *The Gospel of Mary Magdalene*, Jean-Yves Leloup commented on the verses in which Jesus says, "Attachment to matter gives rise to passion against nature. Thus, trouble arises in the whole body; this is why I tell you: 'Be in harmony. . . .' If you are out of balance, take inspiration from manifestations of your true nature." Leloup notes that doctors do not understand this philosophy of nonattachment. "When a physician tries to reassure a dying patient with false optimism, trouble arises—the doctor's attempts create a kind of schizophrenic double bind that can engender more suffering than before," he writes. "The body knows very well what its ultimate destiny is, and a person in this situation is in need of a different kind of word, addressed to something other than that which is ultimately destined to be decomposed."

We remain until we are no longer able to remain in this particular state.

It is time to come to terms with the failure of organized religion to address the spiritual needs of Americans in regard to the meaning of life and death. We are leaving people to the mercy of a medical system that cannot possibly cure people of every disease, especially not of old age. Yet people beg for treatments and cures, resulting in costs for insurance, pharmaceuticals, and hospitals that rise every year.

Doctors are at a loss to help people understand when treatments are of no avail. They will prescribe treatments that not only destroy the quality of a person's remaining days but cost an exorbitant amount both in money and in labor. Only in rare cases will doctors tell a patient who has no hope of recovery to go home, make final plans, call hospice, and enjoy their remaining days to the best of their ability.

One of Brent's doctors, a radiation specialist who was going to treat the lump on his left temple in which they'd found esophageal cells from the surgery more than a year earlier, had a difficult time dealing with death. He was Jewish and was ambivalent about life after death, and certainly he did not believe in reincarnation. He was a quiet man, and a bit down-beat. While he deals with human mortality on a daily basis, I got the feeling that he didn't ever really *deal* with it. He was reluctant to give Brent the analysis of the PET scan: there were numerous spots of cancer throughout his body, not just the one on his temple. However, I think that our reaction surprised him—and put him at ease. We explained our view of death and dying, and how it must be embraced as part of the path. He asked us where this idea came from, opening the door for me to tell him a bit about Buddhism. He was so impressed that when we saw him a few months later, he told us he'd attended a seminar on death and dying given by a Buddhist monk at the local Mayo hospital.

The doctor's partner in the radiation clinic, a Hindu, had a completely different attitude toward life and death. It was interesting to watch these two men in action and how they dealt with patients. Dr. Baht, the Hindu, was more matter of fact. He was very upbeat, even in the face of his dying patients, because, thanks to his Hindu philosophy, he saw death as no big deal. "I'm sixty-nine," Dr. Baht told Brent one day during a treatment. "When I'm seventy, I told my wife I'm going to quit taking vitamins, because there's no point in wanting to live much longer. Seventy is old enough!" He and Brent had a good laugh over that.

Medical ethics should be about helping to alleviate suffering, something that becomes increasingly more important to people as they near death due to chronic illness. Yet too many times doctors have never been taught about death or how to handle the deaths of their patients, so their only aim becomes to keep them alive. As Diane Meier, a leader in the palliative-care movement, writes, "Almost without discussion, the primary moral principle underlying medical practice became the obligation to prolong life regardless of the toll in suffering, poor quality of life, or cost."

In her book *Knocking on Heaven's Door*, Katy Butler goes into great detail about her father's tragic life, which came about as a result of extensive treatments and the installation of a pacemaker that ultimately made her mother's life a living hell as well. "We hadn't created this mess," writes Butler. "My father's drawn-out dying and my mother's suffering were the consequence of our culture's idolatrous, one-sided worship of maximum longevity. As far as I was concerned, this violated the way of the universe and was a moral crime."

Guy Bourgeault comments in *On Being Human* that there are similarities between the Judeo-Christian tradition and the Greco-Roman "heritages" in which human action is necessary to the "filling in the gaps of creation, correcting its errors" and becoming cocreators with God, helping to alleviate human pain and suffering. The world is imperfect, he notes, as many ancient traditions teach. Thus, it is no wonder that when we become sick, Western medicine "progressively concentrates more on the battle to conquer illnesses," writes Bourgeault, than on embracing illness as a part of the spiritual path.

There are still people who believe that disease can be avoided and miraculously cured if only people were more in tune with themselves, more in balance and alignment with the universe. Yet even the most balanced and aligned people fall ill or die at some point. Disease—or dis-ease, as some like to put it—was once thought of as punishment for sin. If one could be free of sin, one could be free of disease. Similarly, people's belief that there was something Brent could have done to cause himself to be cured (because for some reason illness is a sign of a misaligned spirit) irked me to no end. They had good intentions, as Job's friends did when they begged him to think what he could have possibly done to make God angry.

People are human. We all have karma, and we are subject to birth, disease, aging, and death. It's all part of life! Embracing all our life's experiences as the path and accepting death as a part of the path that we are each called to walk is key to having not only a good death but a good life as well.

Part 3

LOOKING
DEEPER
INTO DEATH

13

WHAT NDEs TEACH US

Advancements in medical science and technology allow us to do something that until fifty years ago was not possible: bring people back from the dead. Near-death experiences, or NDEs, are now allowing doctors and scientists—many of whom never believed that life continues after the death of the physical body—to glimpse this other level of consciousness and know that life does indeed go on. NDEs are enabling us to understand how the soul leaves the body and what happens and where we go after. We've gone beyond mere belief in life after death. We are now certain that life continues, but on a different level of consciousness.

Stuart Hameroff, MD, has developed the theory of the superposition of consciousness. From his studies of people under anesthesia and his conversations with them after bringing them out of their anesthetized state, he has learned that there are many levels of consciousness in which we can exist at any given time. We are never unconscious; rather, our mind merely moves from one state of consciousness to another. My own studies of Buddhism, my meditation, and my experience with listening to Brent describe the level of consciousness we call death have confirmed the truth of this idea to me.

Howard Storm, an art professor at Northern Kentucky University, experienced a near-death state while taking students on a tour of art museums in Paris. In his book *My Descent into Death,* he tells of his NDE. Much of what he was taught is also found in *The Tibetan Book of the Dead* and in *The Egyptian Book of the Dead*, which both have remarkably similar teachings, even though they came from two very different parts of the world.

After leaving his body, Storm says he continued to feel his body in a very real way. This is not unusual, as esoteric teachings say that if we are deeply attached to our bodies, it can take quite a while to lose the feeling that we still have them. Storm makes it clear that he was extremely attached to his body, his job, his personality, his status as an artist and teacher, and the things he owned.

Storm writes a great truth: "Everything I had experienced before this was a dream compared to the way that I was now experiencing reality." He talks about a voice "that sounded like my voice but wasn't." I understand that. My inner voice, which I first heard when I was ten years old while sitting in my "thinking tree" by the creek that ran through our farm, has always seemed to be like my voice, but coming from somewhere else inside me. It's my voice, but it isn't. It asks me questions, tells me what to do, and gives me guidance. Although it sounds like my voice, it comes from somewhere externally, in my mind but not *of* my mind, and often surprises me with answers and new ideas. I find myself saying, "Gee, I would have never thought of that!"

This voice may be what is sometimes called our solar angel guardian angel, or spirit guide; I've heard all those terms used by various people. Aunt Geneva, a relative who had clairvoyant abilities and first taught me about reincarnation (although she was reared Mormon, she left that denomination at age sixteen, knowing that her path was much different), had access to speaking with what she called her "spirit guide."

The Bible speaks of a "still small voice" that spoke to the prophet Elijah (1 Kings 19:12). Like Elijah, when I was a child, I called it the voice of God. Now I know that it is of a divine nature, but it is my solar angel or spirit guide. In the Mormon Church, there is a song that goes, "Listen to the still, small voice; listen, listen. When you have to make a choice, listen, listen." How true! One's inner voice is one's best guide to life's path. Some believe it is our Higher Self speaking to our lower self, reminding us of the truth about certain things.

To return to Howard Storm, he gets to the crux of life on this other level of consciousness when he begins to have an experience that most of us might find unusual, given the other NDE stories we've heard. The clue comes from his statement that "my life was devoted to building a monument to my ego. My family, my sculptures, my painting, my house, my gardens, my little fame, my illusions of power were all an extension of my ego."

This is a key point to understand. Ego is the lowest form of the "I." Ego creates the illusions that this world, this stuff, this body is real. In Buddhism and Hinduism, illusion is called *maya*. Often people mistake the word *illusion* as meaning things do not exist. But the concept really means that while things exist and we can perceive them with our senses, they *do not exist in the way we think they do; things are not inherently real from their own side.*

When the soul fell into the body, we became trapped in the illusions that separate us from God. We can choose to buy into the illusions and become proud, vain, materialistic. All we have—our nice cars, our fine homes, our many possessions—are to prop up the ego. Pema Chödrön calls these things "props," like those we might have for a stage play; they're not real, just props for our egos. We become attached to the things that we accumulate, and our attachment to the illusion of their reality causes us to suffer.

Howard Storm learned this truth. The fact that his ego was the driving force in how he lived his life is critical to understanding the experience he had during his NDE, when "cruel, merciless beings" began ripping and tearing at him, screaming at him, and trying to keep him separate from God. Where was the light and the love we read about with so many NDEs? Who were these strange, dark, cruel creatures that attacked Storm?

One answer might be taken from the *Asclepius:* "Now, when the soul comes forth from the body, it is necessary that it meet the demon [which God has appointed to be overseer or judge over the souls of men]. Immediately, the demon will surround this one and examine him in regard to the character that he has developed in his life."

Storm continues: "All of my life, I'd fought a constant undertone of anxiety, fear, dread, and angst." How sad! But this is the result of his feeling of separation from God and from his fellow human beings, and of his strong attachment to the illusion. "I didn't live in the present," he writes. Storm explains who these horrible creatures were:

> How ironic it was to end up in the sewer of the universe with people who fed off the pain of others! I had had little genuine compassion for others. It dawned on me that I was not unlike these miserable creatures that had tormented me. Failing truly to love, they had been led into the outer darkness where their only desire was to inflict their torment onto another. Devoid of love, hope, and faith, they craved intimacy but found it only to be more torment. Any mention of God, whom they had rejected, enraged them. These debased people may have been successful in the world, but they had missed the most important thing of all, and now were reaping what they had sown.

Yes! In that paragraph, Storm has described himself and his attitude toward life. The demons he encountered were himself. He had come face-to-face with his own worst self—his ego. He also discovered that we create our own reality. We create our own heaven and hell. Or as the cartoon character Pogo might say in a variation of that famous comic strip quote, "We have met the demons and they are us!" These demons were Mr. Storm's animal nature, the ego, the selfish self that we cling to when we believe that we are in control. We truly are our own worst enemy.

It was only after confronting his terrifying ego that Storm was allowed to see his true, divine nature. It's tough to see God when our animal nature or ego is in the way. But when we get beyond the outer darkness of our self-created demons, we can enter the light of the divine nature. We can see God!

At that point Storm was embraced by a "loving, luminous being who . . . knew me intimately. He knew me better than I knew myself. He was knowledge [gnosis] and wisdom [*sophia*]." Notice that I have put the ancient esoteric terms for these two traits in brackets. Because of his Judeo-Christian background, he recognized this being as Jesus, who had come to earth to take on the Christ consciousness. Knowledge and wisdom are two of the primary traits of the Christ consciousness.

Storm next mentions that off in the distance, "far, far away," he sees a center that was "an enormously bright concentration of light. Outside the center, countless millions of spheres of light were flying about, entering and leaving that great concentration of light at the center." In the ancient esoteric traditions, God is the divine source or Oversoul, from which all other beings emanate. This great Oversoul (about which Ralph Waldo Emerson often spoke), the source of our being and our divine natures, is pure light, pure love, and pure intelligence. We are merely sparks from this Oversoul, which we call God.

According to some esoteric teachings, this Oversoul emanates the second level of beings, the creator gods (known in Judeo-Christianity as the Elohim, in Gnosticism as the

Demiurge and archons or "architects," and in Theosophy as the Dhyani-Chohans). These creator gods found a way to embody the souls of beings and create the human. As we read in Genesis 1:26, "God said, 'Let *us* make man in *our* image, after *our* likeness.'" The plural shows that there are many creator gods working under the one God or Oversoul.

Storm describes them this way: "In the center of heaven is the One God surrounded by a vast number of beings that have achieved divinity as the children of God. None of them dream for a moment that they are God. They retain their identity united in God. They participate with God in creation."

Storm also notes the importance of thought power. "As a man thinketh, so is he." Everything transpires through thought. That is why even in our physical bodies, thoughts are critical to the well-being of the universe and to our spiritual progress. Thoughts have tremendous power over other people and the earth.

Another universal principle is love and compassion. Storm stresses that God is not interested in anything about our lives except whether or not we've had unconditional love and compassion for our fellow beings, including all sentient beings, not just humans. That is ultimately what this life is about. Love is all—love of self and love of neighbor (as Jesus taught). "It is impossible to love another person if we do not love ourselves," Storm writes. How true!

We are not here to convert others to our way of thinking or believing. We are here for one purpose: to advance spiritually and become one with the Divine Mind. We can do this by demonstrating the pure love, pure light, and pure intelligence of the Divine, of which we are an inseparable part. We can only accomplish this by loving others unconditionally.

Nor are we here to judge one another ("Judge not that ye be not judged": Matthew 7:1). "How we judge people has little to do with how God knows us," Storm writes. "We judge people by their actions, and God knows us by our intentions." This is another great principle taught in many spiritual traditions: intention is everything. We are never to judge another because we do not know their heart or mind—their intention. Intention is always the basis for what we do and how we are judged. "Our lives are our judgment," Storm writes. How true! Ultimately, we will be called upon to judge ourselves. We know where we stand spiritually, and what we need to do, the karmic debts we need to pay. No one else needs to do that job for us.

Storm also talks about karma:

> The principle of cause and effect governs our life experience. God wants us to know this to the very core of our being. Our every thought and every deed have an effect on our sphere of influence. Negative thoughts produce negative actions just as positive thoughts result in positive outcomes.

This was also the point of Mitch Albom's little book *The Five People You Meet in Heaven*. We have an enormous sphere of influence, beyond anything we can ever imagine, which is why we need to be so careful not to create karma for ourselves. We do have to pay our karmic debts: they cannot be avoided.

Sometimes those karmic consequences happen instantly, in this life; sometimes the payment will be delayed until a future life, depending on what we need to learn and when. Karma is a part of every religious and spiritual tradition from eons to the present, and it is like gravity: it exists whether we believe in it or not.

Storm writes that karma is "God's justice . . . we will all reap the consequences of our actions in this world and in the next life," he notes, adding that "it is the nature of God's love to let us reap the consequences of our actions."

I believe that karma is not so much God's justice, but that it is perfect justice, because our karma is self-created. We do not reap the punishments that others might bestow upon us for our misdeeds, but we gain the suffering or the blessings of our own individual choices. That makes justice perfect.

Storm was told (in 1985, when he had his NDE) that "the world is at the beginning of a major transformation. It will be a spiritual revolution that will affect every person in the world." Many in the esoteric community are well aware of this shift. The Institute of Noetic Sciences even has a magazine titled *Shift*. At the beginning of the new millennium, esoteric people all over the world began a march of conscious thought to help this shift take place. It is occurring now, and we can see the results, although many do not know what to look for.

What happens when we die? Everyone asks that question, whether openly, to a minister or spiritual teacher, or quietly, in our deepest inmost self. When we die, writes Storm, "[Angels] will take you from the reality of this physical universe and transport you to a new reality where you get your first introduction to the wonder and power of God. There are as many entry points into heaven as there are individuals. Each person is escorted toward heaven according to his or her life, culture, and spiritual level."

Again, we create our own reality, our own heaven, and our own hell. Notice that he does not say that we will be guided on the basis of the church door we enter on Sunday morning. We will see what we believe through the wisdom eye of our mind.

Storms goes on to discuss our angels or spirit guides. He emphasizes how we need to accept their guidance and listen to our inner voice, no matter how strange it may seem. He also discusses our separation from God, and how this is not our real home. (I call this earthly existence "boarding school" because we are sent here to live and learn, then return to our Divine Source.)

"Hell is separation from God," says Storm. That is why our hell is right here on this earth—not off in some other realm where our souls are sent for eternity. That is not justice, and God is perfectly just. This earth is the place where we experience separation from God.

Both Hinduism and Buddhism teach that nirvana and samsara are not actual places but rather are states of mind. How do you see your life? Your life becomes what you believe it to be. The separation we feel from God or the Divine is created by our own sense of *self* and *other*. That is why it is so important that we do nothing to cause division, create exclusivity, or otherwise cause separation. Even worse is religions that cause separation. Using God to cause separation is the worst form of all.

In the esoteric tradition, it is believed that after the fall of mankind into physical bodies, we gradually became more and more dense. People of Atlantis, Lemuria, and other early civilizations were not as dense as we are. As we became more human and our animal nature more prevalent, we became denser in our physical nature. That is why we are so much more subject to disease and deterioration of the physical body than people were eons ago. As Storm points out, as we grow in Christ consciousness, we grow lighter and brighter, and our bodies become more translucent in nature. This is something ancient esoteric taught us thousands of years ago.

Where do we go upon our death? We all go to "heaven," or to this other level of consciousness; we all are taken to the place that best suits our spiritual level. We encounter the personages in which we have been conditioned to believe. There is no true division on the level of consciousness we call death. We truly see all as one. God loves everyone unconditionally, meaning that God's love is not dependent on which church we go to or even if we go to church. There are no churches in heaven. That will be a hard pill for many to swallow, but as Storm, along with hundreds of others who have had NDE experiences, can attest, religious institutions are a product of man, not God. "Too often we claim God's love for our closest group. We exclude everyone outside the group as being outside God's love. This is opposed to God's will. God loves everyone beyond anything we can imagine," he writes.

Discussing reality, Storm says, "We are the projected children of the mind of God," echoing a view of creation stated in the ancient esoteric traditions such as the Kabbalah. As quantum physicists now know, the entire universe, down to the smallest molecule, is composed of vibratory energy. Storm appears to confirm these findings when he says, "Matter is a state of energy. Energy is the realization of the divine mind. Energy is created in a vibration of the divine mind." That is why healing can be performed by those who focus on our vibratory energy rather than on our physical bodies, which are too dense to be able to receive healing directly.

"It takes time and planning to get energy to a point where it can be brought to a more sophisticated and structured state," writes Storm. These resemble ideas in some of the ancient esoteric writings, which claim that the Elohim had a difficult time developing a body of matter and energy that could contain the soul. We kept slipping out.

Regarding reincarnation, Storm writes, "If the soul fails in the physical, for whatever reasons, it will go back to the source. It may come back into this physical world or another. Were it to come back, which is just one of countless possibilities, it would be more highly developed." Although he is talking about babies who die before birth or young children who die, it is true of all of us. It takes us many lifetimes to become highly enough developed spiritually to become creator gods and experience unity with God.

Storm emphasizes that we cannot know the true nature of reality because our five senses limit us to this reality only. "The religious mysteries direct us toward the true nature of reality that we are unaware," he says. "Religion opens our mind and spirit to the greater reality. When we face the mysteries of our existence, we can surrender our ego and begin to experience more of the greater reality."

Yes, there is a "realer" reality than the one we experience here with our five senses. In Buddhism, meditation is one technique by which we can learn to experience this greater reality. Christian mystics such as St. John of the Cross, Joan of Arc, and many others (some of whom were burned at the stake as heretics by the Catholic church) saw this greater reality in their hours of meditation and wrote and spoke of it.

Perhaps the most telling answer Storm received was to the question "Which is the best religion?" Storm was told, "The religion that brings you closest to God."

"But which one is that?" asked Storm. The answer he received was one that is vitally important to all of us on a spiritual journey: It is not important which religion we adopt or which church door we enter on Sunday—or even if we go to a church. Religion can act as a guide on the path; it can introduce us to a "personal relationship with God." But while religion can offer us a road map, it is "not the destination." Too often, Storm writes, people get stuck in the rigid dogma of a certain religion and they never move beyond to developing their spiritual selves.

Although faith still plays an important part in Storm's life, he gives us to understand that at some point we move beyond faith to a true knowledge of that other reality—who we are, where we came from, and where we are going. If Storm has done anything, he has reaffirmed that this particular level of consciousness is not all there is. There are other, greater realities. Understanding this should help us all have a good death, one without fear, knowing that all things happen for our greater good—even confronting our demons.

14

DYING WITH GRACE AND DIGNITY

Before I became old, I took care to live well; in old age I take care to die well. And dying well means dying willingly

— SENECA

Brent remained a funny guy until the end. At a group lunch one day to celebrate the birthday of a work colleague, everyone was trying to decide what they could order to eat because nearly everyone was on some kind of diet or another. Brent spoke up and said, "Just be glad you're not on my diet—it doesn't have any T in it." It took a few seconds, but suddenly everyone got it, and when Brent began laughing at his great joke, they all began laughing too. He believed that laughter was the best thing in life.

One day, just a couple of weeks before he died, he decided to take his Corvette out for a run on the freeway. It was early in April on a Sunday morning, not much traffic, and he could get it up over 100 mph and have fun. When he came back and told me he had the 'Vette up to 120 on the freeway, I was stunned. "You're going to get a ticket," I told him.

"That's okay," he replied. "I'll be dead by the time I have to go to court." He considered that one of the benefits of being a "short-timer."

At work one day, after getting off the phone with a client—with whom he was laughing while talking business—one of the other salespeople, a young woman, came to him and asked, "How can you have so much fun when you know you're going to die?"

"We're all going to die, Jennie," he said to her. "But I'm one of the lucky ones—I know about when I'm going to die, and I know what I'll die from. That's a luxury most people don't have."

* * *

How true! We all live with the great mystery of how long we'll live and how we'll die. Brent was lucky. He knew however, that it's not how we die that really matters—it's how we live.

We don't often hear stories of people dying with grace and dignity, and especially not with a sense of humor. Too often we hear horror stories of people sent to hospitals, where every effort is made to keep them alive at all costs.

A friend of my mother's called one morning, frantic. Her husband, who had had mouth cancer and had his lower jaw and most of his palate removed, was in the hospital again. For the previous six months he'd been taking nourishment through a feeding tube in his stomach. Now he was in very bad shape, as the cancer had returned, and he was bleeding internally.

"What can I do?" she cried to my mother. "They want to give him many blood transfusions to keep him alive. I don't think they should do that. What can I do?"

My mother told her to tell the doctors what she and her husband wanted. "It's up to you to tell them what to do and what not to do," my mother advised her. "Just tell them no!"

That is what my mother's friend did, and her husband finally died after a terrible struggle.

Another friend of mine told me how hard it was for her family to let their father go. "Everyone was standing around him begging him not to die, saying, 'Don't go, Dad!' and crying and pleading," she related to me. "It was terrible, until finally I told them all to leave the room. I took my father in my arms and held him and told him it was okay to go. He died peacefully."

Another heartwarming story comes from a good friend, who lost his mother in October 2005. When in the summer the doctor told the eighty-five-year-old woman that she had cancer and began talking to her about how her treatment protocol of chemotherapy would commence, she stopped him in midsentence and said, "It must be very difficult for you to have to talk to people about death."

She then explained, with two of her daughters by her side, that she'd lived a good, long life—"I've had a good run," as she put it—and she wasn't interested in making the last months of her life miserable by having chemo. She preferred to go home, go about her life, and when the time came it would come naturally, and her family supported that decision. I can't imagine how relieved that doctor must have been to meet this woman of such strength and grace.

Another friend of mine, whose father is a medical oncologist, told me that his father always says the most difficult thing about his job is not dealing with the patients—often they are accepting and ready—but dealing with the extended family, who insist that the doctor pull out all the stops to save the person they love. Many times, the patient gives in to the family's wishes, thinking that it is better appease them. This doctor says that caving in to the family's wishes, knowing the suffering that the treatment will cause for the patient—sometimes with little hope that treatment will prolong the patient's life—is difficult to face. He's often said he wished that people better knew how to die.

Most of this desire to keep a loved one alive despite the doctor's reluctance to perform further treatment comes from our ego. We have attachments to those we love—egoic attachments, which really have to do with our own desires to keep the person with us rather than with the person's best interests. That is why it is so critical to develop nonattachment. Nonattachment frees us from our own ego desires to have life the way we want it and gives us the freedom to show compassion for the other person. When we can do this, we can allow that person's karmic fate to play out, and we can act in their best interest, which often means just helping them have a good death. It means giving up the struggle to have life the way we want it and allowing it just to be.

Dr. Kevin Haselhorst is an emergency-room doctor at a hospital in the Phoenix area. His book *Wishes to Die For* helps people understand how important end-of-life issues are and how they can develop a healthcare directive so that doctors, hospitals, and the person's family know what the person wishes for in terms of dying.

Haselhorst is calling for a universal healthcare directive, which goes throughout one's life from prenatal and preventive care to advanced care when one becomes ill to palliative care for incurable and end-stage disease. He then takes it one step further to "omega care," in which one goes with the flow, fate makes the decisions, and humility comes into focus.

In a lecture I attended, Dr. Haselhorst said, "Suffering is admirable when there is a cause to get better, not when there is no hope." His personal end-of-life philosophy is: "Leave well enough alone until I'm sick enough to die."

Doctors, some by their own admission, are often incapable of talking to people about end-of-life issues. Much of this has to do with the idea that if a patient dies, someone, or the illness-care system, has failed. But dying is not a failure; it's a natural part of living. Although Medicare is now offering monetary reimbursement for the time a doctor spends talking to patients about end-of-life issues, in an attempt to get their patients to express their wishes about care—doctors, who think of themselves as healers, still find the subject difficult.

In his book *Flow: The Psychology of Optimal Experience*, author Mihaly Csikszentimihalyi describes some techniques we can use to be happy no matter what happens in life. Even if life can become chaotic and out of control, there is a way to turn "adversity into an enjoyable challenge."

Learning to see even adverse events as opportunities for spiritual growth takes patience and practice along the path. Adversity can be transformative if we see the events of our lives as teaching times or motivational moments that can make life a more positive experience. Fighting against adversity often results in more suffering. Csikszentimihalyi says that the "integrity of the self depends on the ability to take neutral or destructive events and turn them into positive ones."

Buddhism refers to this attitude as one of turning all adverse conditions into the path. We cannot judge our situations or conditions as good or bad—they are just situations or conditions we experience in samsara. It is our karma; we must work with it, move with the flow, and, without judgment or preferences, embrace and learn from it as the path. The minute we judge a situation and circumstance as bad, we begin to lose sight of the good that can come from it.

Csikszentimihalyi then provides three clues to why some people are "weakened by stress, while others gain strength from it." The answer, he says, is simply that they know how to turn stressful or hopeless situations into flow experiences. He speaks of "unselfconscious self-assurance. . . . They did not doubt their own resources would be sufficient to allow them to determine their fate. . . . Their energy is typically not bent on dominating their environment as much as on finding a way to function within it harmoniously."

Perhaps this was one of the keys to Brent's well-being in the face of cancer. He was not bent on fighting it, which can have negative implications, as much as he was embracing it or living harmoniously with the disease.

Csikszentimihalyi tells us that one key to learning to live harmoniously or going with the flow, even in adverse circumstances is seeing ourselves as embracing whatever happens, rather than being in constant opposition to it. We don't want to be ill or be part of a communicable disease "pandemic" that we feel threatens us into a fighting stance. Yet this is the environment in which we must operate, and in the face of these adverse conditions, we sometimes "have to be subordinated to a greater entity." To rise above suffering and embrace life as it presents itself to us requires us to "play by a different set of rules" than those we'd typically prefer.

According to Csikszentimihalyi, the person who can successfully navigate adverse events is typically one who "focuses their attention on the external world, not the internal world of the ego." We tend to focus on the self—particularly the physical body and all the feelings that go along with that egoic self, especially pain and suffering. Stress occurs when we feel that we are being threatened either by disease or adverse situations that go against the grain of what we believe we want or don't want, and what should or should not be happening. The result of our resistance to adversity is worry and stress, which takes a lot of energy from us. It's not that we stop focusing on what we want—to be healthy and well—but we must become "open enough to notice and adapt to external events," even if they are not what we want.

This is an important statement. People who tend to focus on their bodies—which are the main focus of the mind for many—generally lean into their fears about illness, which ultimately leads to a fear of death. A shaman healer once said, "Where attention goes, energy flows. Energy flows where attention goes." One can concentrate on physical pain and put all one's energy there, or one can focus on external things— work, enjoying a good book, watching a baseball game—and the energy will go there to the point where the pain is no longer a present reality.

Third, Csikszentimihalyi suggests, leave yourself open to the discovery of new solutions. Be flexible! Perhaps there is no cure for cancer, but be flexible enough to learn to embrace it, to learn from it, and above all, not take it too seriously, as the worst thing that can happen. As Brent liked to say, it was just part of his adventure. It was challenging. It was painful. But he didn't think about it much. He worked every day, and when he was at home, he read magazines and books that interested him, watched sports, got excited about his favorite team winning, got angry at the refs, and so on. "Almost every situation we encounter in life presents possibilities for growth," says Csikszentimihalyi.

Again, as long as one is focused on the way one wishes life would be or what one believes life *should* be or hopes life *could* be, falling into the trap of wanting life to be different than it is, one will be unhappy. That is a Buddhist teaching—that suffering results when one wants life to be other than what it is. The key to living happily is learning to go with the flow—to accept that this is how things are. It just is. That is my biggest challenge—to accept that this is just how life is. I can't change it, but I can embrace it, see it as an adventure, and learn from it.

David Steindl-Rast writes, "Let's learn to die so that, when our last hour comes and if we are still alert to it, we will be able to die well. But at any rate let's learn it, and that means let's learn to give ourselves over and over again to that which takes us; let go of things, or rather give up . . . . Letting go is too passive, . . . giving up is the truly sacrificial gesture. In so many traditions you have this notion that throughout our lives we train for a right dying; that means to train for flowing with life, forgiving ourselves."

Going with the flow of life also means learning to flow into death with the same untroubled ease of accepting that this is how it is supposed to be. We embrace death with the same passion as we embraced life.

Dying with grace and dignity means dying knowing that we have lived a life of meaning and purpose, and can accept our death with peace, having lived a life of intention.

15

CHOOSING DEATH:
SUICIDE AND ASSISTED SUICIDE

Thursday, May 10, 2018, was the day the one-hundred-and-four-year-old Australian ecologist David Goodall chose to die. He had traveled to Switzerland to end his life under that country's laws, which permitted assisted suicide. He granted an interview to a journalist about his decision to choose death.

Goodall was not terminally ill, noted the article by journalist John Miller, but he was ready to die, and assisted suicide was illegal in Australia. His death by lethal injection was scheduled for May 10, and family members would be present, said the article.

"One should be free to choose the death, when death is at an appropriate time," Goodall told the reporter, who noted that he wore a pullover emblazoned with the words "Aging Disgracefully."

On June 5, 2018, the businesswoman and entrepreneur Kate Spade, famous for her purses and other fashion accessories, was found dead in her New York City apartment. She had hanged herself with a scarf (one of her own design, perhaps?). On June 8, 2018, famous globe-trotting chef and author Anthony

Bourdain was found dead in his hotel room in Strasbourg, France, also from hanging.

One day I read several Facebook posts. One was from a Western Buddhist group asking for prayers for a young man who'd committed suicide but didn't give a reason. Another asked for prayers for a young woman who'd committed suicide after a relationship breakup. A middle-aged man killed himself because of financial problems. It made me stop and think—I see a lot of these posts on Facebook.

Suicide rates are on the rise across the United States, increasing by 24 percent from 1999 to 2014. NonHispanic white men commit suicide at the highest rate: 26.5 percent, with Hispanic men trailing at 10.9 percent. White women commit suicide at the rate of 7.9 percent, higher than Hispanic women or black women, according to a 2016 report. These increases were driven, among other things, by mental illness, drug and alcohol abuse, financial hardship, and relationship problems.

Why do people commit suicide? In article after article, psychologists and psychiatrists offer their observations: the more educated commit suicide at lower rates than the less educated; financial difficulties are often the catalyst, but wealthy people commit suicide too; drugs are a major cause—but in many of these cases, who knows if the overdose was accidental or intentional?

Some perhaps feel that death is preferable to continuing a life that is pure hell or even merely unsatisfactory. Before triggering the device that would deliver a lethal dose of a barbiturate, Goodall told a reporter, "My life has been rather poor for the past year or so, and I am very happy to end it."

I thought about that statement. How many of us can say that there have been periods in our lives when things have gone poorly? Of course, most of us weren't one hundred and four years of age, which can add a bit of urgency. Like Goodall, my grandfather's sister, my great-aunt Clara, was one hundred and four when she died. She lived on her own until she was ninety-six before moving into assisted living. When my mother visited her over her last few years, Aunt Clara—a soft-spoken, kind, and patient woman—would tell her, "I think God has forgotten about me."

Days filled with sitting and being unable to read because of poor eyesight, not hearing conversations because of poor hearing, being unable to walk about without fear of falling, leads one to feel that life is, as Goodall put it, "rather poor."

I watched an elderly friend—a published, award-winning writer—go from getting around her house and sitting at her computer for hours, writing every day, to being unable to get around so well, to moving to assisted living, where she still had her precious computer, so she could write.

Then, at age ninety-four, she could no longer get around or care for herself, and she was moved into a nursing home. She was ready to go at that point and wanted to die. She believed that there was nothing after death, so she had no fear of dying. She longed for her computer and lamented daily her inability to write. She longed for death, but it was slow in coming. She had no disease that would take her quickly. She was just old. "Too long, too old," she would tell me on my visits.

My friend began having lots of "visitors" to her room in

the nursing home. She would tell me about all the people that showed up to talk to her and how wonderful it was to have so many visitors every night. Of course, these visitors were from another level of consciousness, coming to keep her company and perhaps to show her there really is an existence beyond this one. After two years in bed in the nursing home, she died.

Is life worth living if one cannot do what one loves to do? If it gets to the point that life becomes "rather poor" in that we cannot actively participate in life the way we wished? When the body begins failing from no specific illness, just old age, frustration often sets in, and the wish to die becomes stronger, as I've observed in many of the elderly friends I've had over the years. If we are merely lingering in a nursing home bed, is life worth it? At that point, is assisted suicide the answer? For everyone that answer is different.

When Bill was diagnosed with advanced stage cancer at the age of 83, the first question he asked his doctor when presented with treatment options was "Will I be able to continue playing golf three days a week?" Bill and his wife, a good friend of mine, were avid golfers. The doctor was honest with Bill telling him that with the treatments he'd be receiving it was doubtful that Bill would be able to play golf ever again. The prognosis was poor. At that point, and in front of his wife, Bill told the doctor that if he couldn't play golf he didn't want to live. His wife, who was 12 years younger than Bill, was stunned at his decision but she could not convince him otherwise. He chose to go home and when things got worse, he entered hospice, dying two months after the diagnosis.

Some believe that refusing medical treatment is akin to committing suicide, but every individual has their way of dealing with life and death.

There are religious stigmas attached to committing suicide. Some believe that it means that one will go to hell in the afterlife. Others believe that it was God who gave us life and only God should take it. (For my great-aunt Clara, God seemed to be a bit slow in that respect.) Others believe that a life of suffering should be cause enough for one to commit suicide or seek assisted suicide. I hear people say, "We put our beloved pets down when they are suffering from illness or old age, why not people?" That is a question still open for debate in the United States. Not so much in Switzerland. Hence David Goodall's final trip to that country to end his own life in peace and comfort, and in dignity.

Choosing the day of one's death is not unusual. It is said that Hindu yogis can choose the day of their death just by declaring it so and using their mind power developed over many decades of training. In the movie *Little Big Man,* each morning the old tribal chief would declare, "Today is a good day to die," before wandering off to sit down and die. Every evening he would return to the encampment, still alive and well. Eventually it happened.

I had a good friend who, along with his wife, belonged to Death with Dignity (formerly the Hemlock Society). They had agreed that when they got old enough and felt that time was up, they would commit suicide together. They'd spent nearly seventy years together and were determined to die together.

But the wife became ill and died suddenly, leaving the husband alone and inconsolable.

During a visit, he wanted to discuss suicide with me. He couldn't talk to his children about it; they would not understand. He asked me what Buddhists thought of suicide. I explained that as a practicing Buddhist, I had no judgment on the matter. Buddhists do, however, teach a lot about pain, suffering, and the alleviation of suffering. While suicide would not be exactly condoned, it would not be condemned either if the intent was to alleviate suffering. "Intention is everything," I told him.

Would there be karmic consequences? There are consequences attached to all our actions, I explained. Ultimately it would be his choice, and I could not judge or tell him what to do.

About a month later, I received an invitation in the mail to this man's memorial service. His daughter had sent out the invitation along with a letter explaining that her father had died unexpectedly on his birthday. I knew then that my friend had chosen the path of suicide. Nothing was ever said; there was no mention of suicide at the memorial service, as it still carries a great stigma.

Suicide often hurts those left behind the most, because they find it difficult to understand why life has become so terrible. That is especially true if the person is young—a teenager or young adult. They seem to be too young to make that kind of permanent choice. Life has its ups and downs, but that is the way life has always been. "Nothing lasts forever," my mother used to say to us kids when we cried about having to go to the dentist. I believe she has always believed that, and it has helped me as well. What comes to us today will be gone soon. Nothing lasts forever, including the bad times in life and the good times. We forget about that part. Yes, even the good times do not last and often turn into suffering.

In Buddhism, happiness is called "changing suffering," because we alternate between extremely happy times, when life seems as if it can't possibly get any better, and the times when that happiness turns into suffering. That new car we saved for because it was the most beautiful car we could imagine and made us feel happy and wealthy suddenly became our source of suffering when it was stolen and wrecked. The person we loved more than anyone in the world—our soul mate, who was our completion—became the person who caused our suffering when they left us for someone else.

Because life in samsara is changing suffering, we can be sure that the source of our unhappiness today will probably change into something different, which will be the source of our happiness tomorrow. Nothing stays the same; nothing lasts forever. The ups and downs of life teach us how embracing all as the path can give us a life of understanding, of compassion for ourselves and for others.

For this reason, some believe that suicide is a selfish act: "I don't want to suffer, so I will kill myself, not realizing that my death will cause others to suffer." Perhaps it is, but I can honestly say that my elderly friend who killed himself after his wife died did so because he could not bear life without her. They had an agreement—a pact—and he was fulfilling his end of the bargain. It was his choice, and it wasn't up to me to judge whether it was a right or wrong choice. Of course, his children and grandchildren suffered, as they were deeply saddened by his death.

There continues to be much controversy surrounding suicide, especially assisted suicide. Some people, like Goodall, choose to go to Switzerland, where assisted suicide is legal. Despite popular belief, not everyone who commits suicide is suffering from a mental illness. Some people are just at what they feel is the end of the line.

There are also feelings of disillusionment, despair, and disenchantment. Life has become something less than we expected it to be. For people who have achieved great fame and fortune, perhaps they expected to feel happier and more satisfied with life. When they failed to achieve it, they became disillusioned.

The road to hell is paved with unmet expectations, I've often said, as life is not always what we had hoped it would be: it is not as exciting, and the future is not as clear or as full of fulfilled dreams.

On the same day that Anthony Bourdain's suicide was announced, Charles Krauthammer, a syndicated columnist and winner of a Pulitzer Prize in 1986 for his outstanding commentary, announced that he had just a few weeks to live. He said that surgery in August 2017 to remove a cancerous tumor in his abdomen resulted in numerous complications. It was discovered that cancer had returned and that his doctors had given him a few weeks to live. "This is the final verdict," Krauthammer wrote in a public letter to friends and colleagues. "My fight is over."

I found it admirable that as others had committed suicide during that week—people who'd lived a good life (or so it seemed), were doing well both physically and financially, chose the path of death over continuing a life of success. Charles Krauthammer, who'd lived nearly all his adult life paralyzed from the neck down but was successful in his own right, chose to live out his life to the end. "I leave this life with no regrets," he wrote. "It was a wonderful life—full and complete with the great loves and great endeavors that make it worth living. I am sad to leave, but I leave with the knowledge that I lived the life I intended."

Those varying situations and outcomes show how suffering is relative, and that a person's state of mind can be different depending on their perspective. To have lived a life in a wheelchair paralyzed from the neck down and call it "a wonderful life" shows that Krauthammer truly had created meaning in his life. He had the courage to live out his life to the end and face dying without regrets or fear, and he lived the life he intended. How wonderful it would be if we could all say that with our last breath!

None of us knows another person's mind and how their suffering—whether we see it as a mental illness or a lucid choice—impacts their will to live or choose death. Perhaps NDEs can allay our fears of death by showing us that we never cease to exist, that mind/soul continues on. People who commit suicide may have more courage than most of us do, and perhaps they fear death less.

Seneca, the Roman Stoic philosopher, wrote much about death and how to die. These writings were compiled and edited by James S. Romm in a little book, *How to Die*, which sheds light on how the ancients saw death, particularly suicide. Seneca felt that suicide was a way to obtain one's freedom from unfortunate circumstances, a means to end one's troubles and to escape slavery. "In every kind of enslavement, the road to freedom lies open. If one's mind is ill and wretched from its own failings, it can make an end of its own sufferings.... Then, if you ask what is the path to freedom, I say: any vein in your body."

Seneca believed that living too long too old is of no use, because the body can no longer function to the benefit of its owner.

> But if one's body becomes useless for performing its functions, is it not fitting to draw the struggling mind out of it? And perhaps, the deed must be done a little before it ought, lest, when it ought to be done, you're no longer able to do it. And when the danger of living badly is greater than that of dying soon, only a fool would not buy his way out of a great risk at the price of a small moment of time. A very long old age has brought few men to death's threshold without debilities, whereas for many, life lies there motionless, unable to make use of what makes it life. Do you think there is anything crueler to lose from life than the right to end it?

Admittedly, in Seneca's time, suicide was considered an honorable thing to do. In fact, Seneca himself committed suicide in AD 65, after being implicated in an unsuccessful plot to assassinate the insane emperor Nero.

Even in the present time, I think it's the circumstances surrounding suicide that make it a tragedy or something more acceptable. When a teenager, who has hardly had an opportunity to explore life, commits suicide, it seems much more grievous than it does for an elderly person who has lived a full and long life and now, feeling its completion, leaves it on his or her own terms.

Contemplating the suicides of two famous, wealthy people (Bourdain and Spade) within a span of a week—people who seemed to have everything to live for—we can perhaps cut them some slack after reading Seneca's reasoned approach to suicide. It truly is, after all, a choice we have to end our suffering, whatever we perceive that to be, even if no one else can understand it.

Seneca didn't have a problem living into old age as long as his mind and body were intact. I think most of us can understand that way of thinking. Many elderly people that I've befriended over my lifetime have some measure of contentment with old age as long as they can have a few enjoyments such as eating, friendships, being able to walk and talk, and especially think and ponder the world. When those things begin to go, people become adamant about wanting to die. Seneca says that when old age "begins to destroy my mind and to tear away parts of it, if what is left to me is not life but mere breath, I'll jump out of the rotten and collapsing building."

For some people, just being able to wake up in the morning and breathe is life enough. I do not think that would be true for me. I think about my writer friend, who was forced to leave behind her computer and her ability to write to lie in bed in a nursing home, lamenting that she could no longer do what she desired to do most. The worst of it was that she was not sick in any way, just old, so it seemed to be a trap, holding her body hostage to old age much longer than something that would kill her quickly.

"I won't use death to escape illness, so long as the illness is curable and does not occlude my mind," wrote Seneca. "I won't use my hand against myself merely on account of pain; to die for that reason is to admit defeat. But if I know that my condition must endure forevermore, I'll leave, not because of the pain itself, but because it will cut me off from everything that gives one a reason to live. It's a weak and idle man who dies on account of pain, but it's a fool who lives for pain's sake."

As sentient beings, our primary concern is realizing happiness and avoiding suffering. Suicide may be a way to avoid unwanted suffering. Fear of death keeps us attached to this level of consciousness we call samsara; it keeps us attached to these bodies, sometimes even when they have stopped serving us. All life is, said Seneca, is a "journey toward death." Perhaps those who commit suicide are much more courageous than those who cling to life just for the sake of breathing. We cannot judge those who choose death over life, because we do not walk in their shoes.

16
DYING CONSCIOUSLY

If you would indeed behold the spirit of death, open your heart wide unto the body of life.

For life and death are one, even as the river and the sea are one.

—KAHLIL GIBRAN, *The Prophet*

Death remains the great mystery of life. That is true to an even greater extent today than it was a thousand years ago. Death was more visible in the past because it was very much a part of the lives of everyday people. Infants died at a terrible rate—as did many mothers giving birth—and no one knew why.

I remember visiting an old graveyard while vacationing in North Carolina many years ago. The graves held the bodies of people who had died in the late 1700s and early 1800s. One section, cordoned off by an iron fence, held nearly a dozen graves. It was a family burial site that held, in addition to several adults, the graves of seven children, all of whom died before the age of two.

Families who lived in rural areas had family grave sites where several generations of the family were buried. I remember visiting one of these sites on a neighboring farm when I was a teenager; I'd found the verses on the tombstones extremely beautiful. A headstone marking the grave of a young woman who died at the age of eighteen read:

> Sweet was the flower
> But short was the bloom,
> It withered here
> For an early tomb.
> But faith forbids
> The sorrowful sigh;
> She withered here
> To bloom on high.

Death prior to the age of modern medicine was very close. The dead were nearby and remembered often. Rituals included the family members preparing the body for burial and sitting up with the body, which was often laid out on the dining-room table or the sofa for three days, until the soul had time to take its leave. Then the body was buried in a grave dug by the hands of relatives or neighbors, sometimes in a wooden coffin built by a local carpenter.

Today death is nearly invisible. It happens in the putrid halls of nursing homes, where the atmosphere of dying hangs heavy, especially to those who work there. It happens in palliative-care rooms in hospitals or hospice facilities. Rarely does it happen at home, in the presence of loved ones gathered round the bed-side of the person taking his or her last breath. Funeral homes handle the body, taking it away to be prepared by professionals for the viewing (if one chooses that), burial, or cremation.

To some degree, the hospice movement has taken us back to the days when death was open, and family members and loved ones gather to say their farewells. Here the medical system is for the most part taken out of the picture. The end of this life-time is as important and miraculous as the beginning. It truly is a time to celebrate the life—and the death—of the person. Some traditions hold wakes, which provide a time for this cele-bration, which is really a celebration of the person's life.

Meditating on our own death, in the Buddhist tradition, teaches us how to die consciously and with intention. I believe that at some point, perhaps when we are nearest to leaving our physical bodies, we are extremely conscious of our death. We come to see ourselves and our life for what it truly was, and if we have any regrets, it's time to let those go; if we have any attachments, we need to release those and go gently into the light.

Sri Aurobindo's companion teacher, the Mother, said, "What happens after death depends absolutely on the condi-tion in which one dies and on his last wish, also on the resolu-tion of his psychic(mind) being. "There is something we can do to help determine our path after death: to die consciously by stabilizing our mind and fixing it on spiritual thoughts that comfort us and take away the fears. Perhaps it is mentally recit-ing or having someone read your favorite scripture, such as the Twenty-third Psalm. Above all, one should avoid having a mind of attachment to this life and the things one has accumulated, or harboring regrets about things not accomplished.

The Eastern traditions teach that if the dying person is conscious, she should try to focus her mind on her spiritual progress rather than on the things of this world and should allow herself to release earthly desires and attachments. Conscious dying requires us to have a steadfast awareness of our impending death and to be ready to leave this level of consciousness, including our loved ones, our accumulation of material things, and our hobbies, to leave behind all that we thought was real and ready ourselves for the realer reality that is the invisible unknown world beyond.

SUFFERING IN THE DYING PROCESS

As we have seen, suffering is in many ways a choice. It is the result of our attachments that we develop in this life, and we can learn not to suffer in death, as we can learn not to suffer in life. Dying does not have to be about suffering, but perhaps the suffering people experience at the time of their death is a cleansing process. Maybe it is something that we need to experience in the final moments before we leave our physical bodies.

I've often heard people speak of meaningless suffering and question why we suffer. As one of my Buddhist teachers used to say, "Pain sometimes is not a choice. Whether or not we suffer is a choice." One could protest that statement: "I would never choose to suffer!" Yet every day we choose suffering by refusing to see clearly with the wisdom mind that all is maya; all is illusion, because nothing exists inherently, from its own side. We suffer most from our attachments, particularly attachment to our bodies, which is why the dying process is so difficult. We may be told over and over that we are *not* our bodies! Yet we don't believe that when confronted the specter of death.

Brent said to me just before he died, "If anyone asks you if I suffered, tell them no, because I never wanted my life to be different than it is." He was able to embrace the suffering as a part of his path; never for one moment was he angry or resentful of it. He found a peace in the dying process because he was always at peace with his life.

For many years I thought that euthanasia was a good thing for those who wanted to die quickly and painlessly. After all, I reasoned, we euthanize our pets when they are sick beyond recovery. Shouldn't we do the same for our loved ones? Yet after spending several weeks watching Brent embrace his own death in our home, I came to know that the dying process and even the suffering that comes with it is not meaningless, at least for some people. There is meaning and even purpose in the dying process.

Watching Brent die, I came to believe that the dying process has purpose: it gives us a way to leave this life gently, consciously, with those who love us by our side. I began to suspect that those who die suddenly and unexpectedly, through an accident or heart attack, might have a more difficult time accepting the loss of their physical body.

I recall reading of a well-known man in our city who was driving home late on a Saturday afternoon after playing a round of golf with friends. He had dinner plans that evening with his wife, but he never made it. While stopped at a red light, he had a heart attack and died instantly. That way of dying reminded me how important it is to take time to meditate on our own death. Death is certain; only the time is uncertain, says Buddhism. We need to be prepared every minute of every day to accept our death graciously and consciously.

Suicide typically does not give one the time to make the transition—much of which happens on this level of consciousness—unless one has actually contemplated it, as my friend did. Yet I can't help but believe that much is lost when one ends one's life quickly. Even so, for many, the continued suffering of this lifetime is worse than death. I believe that they will continue to work things out in the *bardo* or wherever our minds/souls go after death.

Embrace life. Embrace death. That's the key to happiness in the Buddhist sense. Embrace whatever we encounter in life. Learn the lessons we need to carry through to our subsequent lives. As we have seen, it helps to believe in karma. It is the ultimate form of justice. If we believe in a just God, then we must believe in karma.

Suffering is inherently part of life in the physical body. We need to know suffering and the causes of suffering: our own attachments, hatred, and ignorance of the way all phenomena exist. To understand as God, or the Absolute, understands compassion, kindness, pleasure, and liberation from our attachments results in freedom from suffering.

Can I ever hope to be as fearless as Brent? I do not know the answer to that. We are all different. We each have our own path in life. I want to believe that the path I walk is the one I need to learn and grow, and is one that will ultimately make me fearless, or at least transform my fear into faithfulness.

DYING IS EASY

On Wednesday morning, I was sitting beside the hospital bed that the hospice had put in the family room. "How easy it is," Brent said all of a sudden.

"What's easy? Dying?" I asked him.

"Yes," he replied softly. "Dying is so easy. I thought it would be harder than this. But it's so easy."

"That's probably because you're not afraid to die," I told him. "People who are afraid to die have a terrible time dying. It's easy for you, just as your life was easy, because you were never afraid."

Several times he looked up and asked, "Am I dead yet?"

"No, not yet," I'd reply.

"Oh, I thought I was dead."

"No, you're not dead yet," I reassured him. "Besides, if you have to ask me whether or not you're dead, it's a pretty safe bet that you're not!" I laughed.

He nodded and smiled, drifting off into that other realm, eyes half-closed as if in meditation. He was seeing many things, but not of this world. He smiled and moved his lips as if talking to someone there. He had smiled so much during the past two weeks.

"You're happy," I said to him.

"Yes, I'm happy," he said, smiling at me.

Later that afternoon he called out to me when I was in

my office, working. I went to him. "I thought I was dead," he remarked.

Hockey was playing on ESPN. "Why don't you watch hockey?" I said.

"Well," he concluded, "I guess since technically I'm not dead, I can watch hockey."

"That's right," I assured him. "Technically you're still alive, so you can watch hockey."

I laughed, and he grinned a big grin.

We had a good day. Wednesday night was difficult. He was restless, moving a lot. I knew from reading and from talking to the hospice nurse that it was another sign that the transition was near. I began sleeping on the leather sofa in the family room on Monday night, just a few feet from where we'd put the hospital bed so I could be near him. He was dry. I put a plastic bowl full of ice chips near him so he could reach over and get some. Every hour I got up and fetched more ice chips from the freezer. He was having a difficult time, and I began hoping that it wouldn't be much longer. It was heart-wrenching to see my best friend—the person I loved most in the world—suffer like this. But I stayed strong. I knew that I'd been called to do this, so I would do what I needed to do to help him.

On Thursday morning, April 29, he kept saying, "I'm leaving. I can't do this anymore!" He kept repeating that over and over. "Goodbye," I'd say to him. To which he'd reply, "I love you. Bye!"

He'd then drift off into his semiconscious state for a few minutes, then ask me, "Am I dead yet?"

"No, not yet," I'd tell him. Then he'd begin saying, "Goodbye, I'm leaving. I love you" over and over.

"Goodbye, I love you too," I'd reply.

"I've learned so much from you," he whispered to me.

"And I've learned so much from you too," I replied.

At about four o'clock that afternoon, he breathed his last breath and transitioned to another state of mind.

* * *

At Brent's memorial service, which I held for his coworkers and his Corvette Club friends, I read this lovely passage on death from Kahlil Gibran's *The Prophet*:

> If you would indeed behold the spirit of death, open your heart wide unto the body of life.
>
> For life and death are one, even as the river and the sea are one.
>
> In the depth of your hopes and desires lies your silent knowledge of the beyond;
>
> And like seeds dreaming beneath the snow your heart dreams of spring.
>
> Trust the dreams, for in them is hidden the gate of eternity.
>
> Your fear of death is but the trembling of the shepherd when he stands before the king whose hand is to be laid upon him in honor.
>
> Is the shepherd not joyful beneath his trembling, that he shall wear the mark of the king?

Yet is he not more mindful of his trembling?

For what is it to die but to stand naked in the wind and to melt into the sun?

And what is it to cease breathing, but to free the breath from its restless tides, that it may rise and expand and seek God unencumbered?

Only when you drink from the river of silence shall you indeed sing.

And when you have reached the mountain top, then you shall begin to climb.

And when the earth shall claim your limbs, then you shall truly dance.

Thich Nhat Hanh, in his book *No Death, No Fear,* says that just because something is no longer manifest does not mean it is no longer real. "It is not because it has not manifested or has ceased its manifestation that you can call it non-being. 'Being' and 'nonbeing' cannot apply to reality. By looking deeply, you realize that reality is not subject to birth and death, to being and nonbeing." The body does not give up the ghost, but the mind/soul chooses to leave the body when the body can no longer sustain it or when progress can no longer be made.

We remain until we are no longer *able* to remain in this particular state. We remain until our purpose here is fulfilled.

That is the way I've learned to think of Brent, and of all things on this level of consciousness: all is either manifest or unmanifest. All exists on some level of consciousness. Those we love and lose are merely unmanifest—but they still exist, and we will meet them again in the next life. Mind or soul is eternal. We are immortal beings experiencing mortality in this physical body, which is just a vehicle that serves us in this particular space-time existence.

I've told various people many times in recent years on my visits with them—dear elderly friends who knew that death was near—that dying is easy. Brent had told me that. All we need to do is lean into the light of consciousness, which takes us to the experience of release. Life continues—it just continues in a different way and in a different consciousness. But it continues to exist, nonetheless.

OM MUNI MUNI MAHA MUNIYE SOHA.

17

THE DYING PROCESS: HAVING A GOOD DEATH

The great transition which death occasions is not from life to death, but from life to life.

—DIANA L. ECK

What does it mean to have a good death? Can dying ever really be good? After studying the dying process and experiencing it with Brent and with several friends over the past few years, I've concluded that a good death is one in which we get to die on our own terms, embracing the process and the inevitability that all beings who are born must die. A good death is a death without fear, without clinging to the material world, and without anger. Brother David Steindl-Rast writes, "I suppose the death we call bad is the one in which we struggle and cannot die peacefully . . . perhaps [the patient] never learned to let go, so he hangs on for dear life, . . . he has not learned to give himself freely. . . . when we really give up and actively die, we die not into death but into a richer life."

Unless our karma creates the conditions for a sudden death, many of us will experience the process of dying—which can last several days or even weeks—and the death of the physical body.

The process seems to remain a mystery to most people, even doctors and nurses and other healthcare providers. Many do not even recognize the signs of impending death and attempt to keep treating the person if he or she is in the hospital. If we're lucky, we'll call on a hospice organization. Although they do not claim to know what happens after death, they do understand the dying process, much of their information coming from sources similar to the Buddhist understanding of dying and death.

Not everyone is fortunate enough to have a peaceful death with loved ones who can help guide the process, because most people in the West do not understand the dying process and because fear sets in as their loved one is dying. Too often people fear dying and what is happening to the dying person, because they do not understand it. Often the ego is involved, as people fear being alone or without their loved one. That is why the practice of nonattachment is so important, not only for our own dying process, but allowing the person we love to leave without our ego interfering with their process.

Death involves a lifetime of preparation—of learning to live well so that we can die well, consciously and embracing the process, going with the flow as our consciousness begins to move from the level of the physical body to a higher level, much as we move from our waking state to a dream state when we fall asleep.

The dying process involves two phases, according to Buddhist philosophy: the outer dissolution, "when the senses and elements dissolve," and the inner dissolution, in which the "senses and elements dissolve," according to *The Tibetan Book of Living and Dying* by Sogyal Rinpoche. Dying people will begin to lose their hearing consciousness and sight consciousness, only hearing as if from a great distance and seeing more from an inner sight than with the physical eyes, which are often closed.

I noticed that as Brent got closer to death, he no longer wanted to keep his eyes open. The day before he died, I turned on the TV so he could watch the hockey playoffs, but when I checked on him later, I noticed that he was lying quietly with his eyes closed. I knew that his eye consciousness was fading.

During death, the life force—the prana or élan vital—settles into the heart chakra, where the mind resides. This process involves, first, the loss of the body's water element. Because our bodies are made up of approximately 55 percent water (for adult women) and 65 percent water (for adult men), we begin losing that element as the dying process advances.

Perhaps the most difficult thing for me to watch was when Brent began losing the water element. Per the hospice nurse's instructions, I had a bowl of ice chips next to him on a table that he could reach.

During the last night, I was sleeping on the couch near his hospital bed. I awoke as he reached for ice chips. When I got up to attend to him, I saw that he was drooling, slobbering uncontrollably. His facial skin, especially his lips, were dried and drawn with wrinkles, as were his hands and arms. This big, two-hundred-pound man had, over the past month, shriveled into a thin, wrinkled body (the earth element), which was now losing the last of its water.

As the fire element began leaving him the day before he died, the warmth began retreating from his hands and arms, feet, and legs, until they were nearly ice cold, yet he removed the cover I had over him because he felt hot. I felt his chest over his heart chakra, and it was extremely hot. I knew that his body's heat had retreated. In spite of the oxygen he'd been on for the past several days, it was becoming increasingly difficult for him to breathe. The air element was leaving too.

The process of helping someone you love have a good death requires the practice of nonattachment, of transcending your own ego in order to allow the person to be at peace during this transition period. It is recommended that anyone attending a dying person be quiet to allow them a period of reflection as the movie of the present life—all of the person's experiences and actions—begins to pass through their mind. Do not disturb the person or touch them on any part of their body, except the crown of their head, which helps to draw the mind/soul upwards to exit—the reverse of how it entered at birth.

According to the *Tibetan Book of Living and Dying*, the Buddhist masters speak of the "need to die consciously with as lucid, unblurred, and serene a mental mastery as possible." Here is where our practice of nonattachment, nongrasping, and desirelessness benefits us greatly. We want to be able to die in a state of contentment and peace, not clinging to our physical bodies or yearning to stay in this life because we love our possessions. It is said that if we die with the desire for our bodies and possessions on our mind, we will have a more difficult time exiting our bodies, and a more difficult time in the in-between state prior to taking rebirth.

Scholar of religions Diana L. Eck says, "Death is dangerous because it is a time of transition. It is a luminal or marginal time, a space between life and life. In this transitional period, the soul is called a *preta,* literally one who has 'gone forth' from the body but has not yet arrived at its new destination." This is why all spiritual traditions have funeral rites.

It is said that just before dying, the person experiences a period of lucidity, with full consciousness of the lifetime they have just lived. It is important that the person not be disturbed during this time; friends and family members in attendance should be quiet observers of this process and not do any loud talking. Often people believe that the dying person cannot hear them because the person appears to be unconscious, but that is not true. It is said that the dying person can hear very well, even if they are not responding. This period of conscious lucidity is very important to the transition, which will be followed by the shedding of the physical sheath.

"Death is not only a time of danger, for it is also said to be a time of great illumination," writes Eck. "At death, they say, the light is very intense, and what separates this shore from the far shore is almost transparent. The time of death, therefore, is a time of clear seeing, of vision, of insight."

At this point, the Buddhist tradition says that the person needs to keep their thoughts on higher beings such as one's guru, the Buddha, or on God, if one is a Christian, because, according to Eck,

> what one thinks and sees at the time of death directs one's first steps toward the next life. While death may be the

final event in one life, it is also, in a sense, the first event in the life beyond. For Hindus, death is not the opposite of life; it is, rather, the opposite of birth. The great transition which death occasions is not from life to death, but from life to life.

"The physical body is a necessary but disposable tool discarded at an appointed time when its particular purposes have been served whether occurring early or late in the person's life," writes Eileen Armstrong.

People in the presence of the dying person need to understand that dying is, or can be, easy, and they must be in accord with the person's journey. One important aspect of hospice training is learning how to help the loved ones, who may be very distraught or fearful of the person's transitioning process. Many times, they will cry and beg the person not to leave them or say things such as "I can't live without you." This can cause the dying person to be upset at the need to leave the physical body and to be reluctant to let go.

Death is an individual process, and each of us must go through it alone. No one can die for us. We must experience it for ourselves. While we may feel the loss of the person's physical presence, we must realize that the person, while not physically manifest, remains spiritually present. Helping our loved ones have a good death is the best gift we can give them, allowing them to experience the release of their body quietly and peacefully.

Part 4

WHAT
HAPPENS
AFTER DEATH

18

KARMA, REINCARNATION, AND REBIRTH

I've often thought how much easier life—and death—would be if everyone believed in the teachings of Buddhism. Since my entrance onto this path, I have had many realizations of what life is, how and why we and all phenomena exist. Through the practice of nonattachment and impermanence, I have become free from fear and know that what we perceive with the five senses is really only created in the mind by the mind, and that mind is all there is. When I hear some people talk of the "mind of God" I am reminded that God is nothing but mind! All is mind; mind is all. All is perfect.

That is what my friend Mal, who was bedridden and on hospice care, told me every time I visited with him: "Remember, Clare, all is perfect." He was determined not to die until he knew everything about life, and I like to think that at his last breath he received the realization that he had sought throughout his eighty-nine years.

The first understanding we must gain is that of karma; unless we understand it, we cannot possibly understand life after death, reincarnation, or rebirth. As a child living happily on a small farm with a loving family who saw to it that the needs and often the wants of my two brothers and I were met, I often wondered how I lucked out, while some of the poor tenant-farmer kids I knew in school barely had enough to eat or clothes to wear. Because I was reared to believe in a kind, loving, all-powerful God, it just didn't make sense to me.

On Mission Sundays at the church we attended, we would often be shown a movie sent to us from Africa by a missionary family our church helped to support. The movie was a bit depressing, as it showed African children living in poverty without much food and with few clothes, minimal medical care, and little schooling. I felt bad for these children and recognized that for some reason I was given a life that was far different. Why? Didn't we as Christians know that God loves everyone equally? But if that was true, why was there so much inequality in the world?

Nothing satisfied those questions until I read Alan Watts's *The Way of Zen* at the age of forty-five and realized that karma played a huge role in who we are, where we are, and why we are, with the life we have. It wasn't God playing favorites; it was our actions in past lives and present; it is the choices we have made over many lifetimes, and the choices we make in this lifetime. Perhaps, I began thinking, God set the universe in motion, and now sits back and watches the movie while our lives play out on this grand stage in exactly the way they are supposed to.

While most people reared in the Christian tradition believe that we reap what we sow, I've come to realize that most do not take that idea literally. It is far easier to believe that it is Satan doing bad things to us. After all, God is all-loving, all-kind. Yet some many people, like the lady I met in Lake Geneva, wonder why God does them harm and cry out to him in anguish when life turns painful. Many people say they can't believe in karma because they can't possibly buy into the idea that we have all created the lives we have.

People often fear the unknown of the life beyond death because they have been taught that we will suffer the horrors of hell if we do not obey the laws of God and the church. The threat of hell is hung over our heads to encourage us to do good (which hasn't worked out too well). In times past, church authorities went into great detail about the horrors of hell in an effort to make people so afraid that they would remain with the church.

Buddhism too teaches about hell. One morning the *sangha* (community) I used to attend received a phone call from a seeker looking for a religion that didn't teach that there is a hell. The sangha's spiritual leader at that time, Kadam Michelle, told him that not only do Buddhists believe in hell, but they believe in many hells. Of course, we in the class where she recounted this event all laughed.

Hence it is very important to understand the mind and consciousness. Both hell and heaven (or nirvana, in Buddhism) are states of mind. To be afraid to die for fear of hell can be seen as totally unnecessary when one realizes that everything in this physical universe and on other levels of consciousness is created in the mind by the mind. So if you don't want to experience hell—either in earthly life or after death—don't create it! We create hell through the actions of the body, speech, and thoughts. How do we create heaven? We create heaven through the actions of body, speech, and thoughts.

Nearly all spiritual traditions have a doctrine regarding eternal life, whether that is a physical resurrection of the body and an eternal life spent in heaven with God, or hell, if one should be judged as deserving of that eternal punishment, as the Christian religion teaches, or taking a "deserving" reincarnation in some material form. It's part of human nature to want to believe that in some way we will live forever in some form. Perhaps that desire to live forever drives our fear of death. We cannot know for certain that what we are will survive the death of the body, because it is extremely difficult to believe that we exist without it. Although religion gives us hope that an eternal life is true, that the "I" has an existence beyond this level of consciousness, that hope sometimes is not enough to assuage the fear of death.

According to Sri Aurobindo, this fear of death is a holdover from our animal origins. Some esoteric traditions teach that our mind/soul has taken a path through all forms of materiality on the physical plane: minerals, plants, insects, animals, and finally human—the highest. This evolution gives us the experience of moving from nonsentient being to sentient and ultimately to super sentient being—the sense of "I" and the ability to make moral choices. The last goal for the human mind/soul is to conquer this fear of death in a conscious, meaningful way that gives us peace throughout our lives.

I had an elderly friend who did not want there to be another life of any type. The thought of a reincarnated life, in which she might be forced to live on this earth again, was especially abhorrent to her. "I'm done with this whole thing," she used to tell me, even though she'd had a reasonably good life in the grand scheme of things. She married well to a man who loved her dearly, had two children (but lost several during her child-bearing years—something for which she could never forgive God, leading her to be certain there is no God), and became an award-winning author of children's books. But her father had died when she was just a child, and she never liked her mother—hated her, actually. During her whole life (she was in her early nineties when we became friends) she never got over this hatred or forgave her mother for getting remarried, multiple times after her father's death, to men that were far less than her father had been.

We spent a lot of time talking about death and what might be afterwards. She did not fear death. Because she didn't believe in an afterlife, she had no fear of being judged, sentenced to some place unpleasant, or forced to face the terrible prospect of taking rebirth. I encouraged her to forgive her mother and enjoy some peace about that part of her life. Over the seven years I knew her, she did manage to soften a bit on the subject. She died just before her ninety-eighth birthday. I often wonder if she was surprised. Or if, as the Eastern philosophies teach, our minds create our own reality, possibly she found exactly what she was expecting—nothing.

Many Christians find comfort in the idea of an eternal life in heaven with God and perceive the idea of returning to another life in another body to be repugnant. But the Christian tradition promotes the idea that we have one life, and there is only one shot at getting it right to ensure an eternal life in heaven. I've often thought that this is what creates a fear of death among Christians—how do you know you've gotten it right and will be judged worthy to go to heaven? What if you've missed the mark, and hell, with its eternal tortures, will be your destination?

I feel sad for those who believe that there is just one life and nothing more. I firmly believe that dying would not be the tragic event that we in the West make it out to be if we knew deep in our hearts that life goes on, that death is just the other side of the coin. The minute we take our first breath, we begin to die. We need to walk through life holding that thought. Birth, death, and reincarnation or rebirth form the great cycle of existence. As Seneca said, "Life is a journey toward death."

In Buddhism, liberation (rather than the Christian idea of salvation) comes when we have "deliverance from the round of successive deaths and births in a perpetual voyage comprising numerous painful incidents, in the course of which we are united to that which we detest and separated from that which we love," writes the famous scholar of Buddhism Alexandra David-Neel. This deliverance, nirvana, is the annihilation of the ego, which is what holds mistaken views or false views or ignorance of how things truly are. David-Neel writes that the Tibetans have no translation for *nirvana*, but their equivalent term is the phrase "gone beyond suffering."

Belief in reincarnation is catching on in the West. Many people (even 24 percent of Christians, when surveyed by the Pew Forum on Religion and Public Life) say they believe in reincarnation. Possible they believe in it because of the many stories of NDEs in the media because they've had such an experience or personally know someone who has, or because they have had some past life recalls themselves.

When my youngest son was eight years old, I received a call from the police department. I was at work, and I'd like to say that the call surprised me, but it didn't. It seems that my son had gone down the street with a friend, found some matches on the hostess stand of a restaurant, and started a fire near the elevator of the two-story strip mall.

Exasperated was a good word for the way I felt. Since his birth, which was not easy and nearly resulted in the deaths of both of us, he seemed to have a self-destructive streak. The doctors told me that they had a difficult time getting him to take his first breath. "It was like he didn't want to live," the doctor told me.

That was just the beginning of his struggle to cope with life. Even at the age of three, he began telling me he didn't want to be here; he didn't want to live. From time to time, he would tell me, "I'm going to kill myself." It was difficult to believe that he would say such things at such a young age.

After I'd picked him up from the police station, I called the only person I knew who could help me: Aunt Geneva, my husband's aunt, who was clairvoyant and was closely connected with her spirit guides. At that time this was an alien concept for me and not in alignment with my Christian upbringing, but I knew that I needed to talk to her. I called her and told her of my son's latest escapade. I asked her if she could help me understand what was going on with this child, who just didn't seem to want to live and was constantly doing self-destructive things.

A few days later Aunt Geneva called. She told me that she'd contacted her spirit guides, and they explained to her that my son had committed suicide in his most recent former life, and he really didn't want to be here. He'd resisted greatly at his birth but was forced to remain here and work out his karma in this life. She then told me that "a grandfather" (she wasn't told which one) would come to him to help him from the other side.

Trying to think who in the Goldsberry family would have committed suicide in their previous life, my inner voice came on: "Bryan is the reincarnation of his grandmother." A lot made sense after that revelation. Bryan's grandmother on his dad's side committed suicide in 1959, leaving four children from ages four to sixteen. The family never knew whether it was a purposeful act or an accident from taking too many sleeping pills because her life had hit a rough patch and she was working long hours to support herself and her children.

That was the answer I'd been looking for. I called Bryan's dad and told him what Aunt Geneva had said about him and what had been revealed to me.

"So many things make sense now," he said. "It explains so many of the feelings I've had about Bryan since he was born."

I've read various theories about suicides. Some say that suicides don't get to spend as much time in the Bardo and must come back sooner. If that is true, the entity (his grandmother) that returned as Bryan was in the Bardo state for only eighteen years before Bryan was born, and perhaps that was not enough. Bryan's life as a teenager was often a struggle and he seemed to attract suicidal energy, including friends who committed suicide. One of Bryan's best friends shot himself at a party of a group of teenagers—a horrible tragedy.

On the day of Bryan's best friend's funeral (who shot himself at a teenage party at the age of sixteen), I explained to Bryan what I'd learned from Aunt Geneva and what had been revealed to me by my own spirit guide, and it seemed to offer him some peace. A few years later, another friend shot and killed himself. Bryan's life has not been easy, as the suicidal energy seems to stay with him, but he's happy, and I believe that knowing that he chose to return (or that his karma impelled him to) has given him a reason for why he is who he is. And perhaps that is enough to get him through.

We do not like to think of the finality of who we are at death, and I believe that all of us on some level want to know that something survives death. Perhaps that is Mind, which, according to Buddhism, is the storehouse of all our karma of body, speech, and mind throughout all our lifetimes. This Mind or soul is a part of the All That Is—the great Mind or the Akashic field, where all information is stored. Scientists say we live in an informed universe, a universe from which we receive all our information.

"After death there is a gradual progression through several states of consciousness varying in length according to the [karma] of the deceased person," writes Eileen Armstrong. We experience the memory not only of this most recent lifetime, but also of other past lives as we integrate and realize their meaning. "The after-death states totally depend on the contents of the life just completed and on the amount of spiritual experience to be digested," says Armstrong. "A lot of time between lives involves reflecting on the spiritually meaningful experiences we have had that expanded our Divine Consciousness."

It is said that our karma, our immortal identity, including traits and personality features, will be stored in the cosmic Mind as seeds that will be the basis for future existences. We are creating our future lives in this present lifetime, and death offers us an entrance into yet another opportunity for spiritual advancement.

Sri Chinmoy says that when we live in the soul, "there is no such thing as death. There is just a constant evolution of our consciousness, our aspiring life. . . . The soul does not forget to carry with it the essence of the experiences that it acquired while it was in the land of the living. While taking its rest, it assimilates the essence of its past. When the assimilation is over, it starts to prepare itself for a new journey." Birth and death are inseparable. They are the two covers of the book whose contents we call life.

BIBLIOGRAPHY

INTRODUCTION

Hermes Trismegistus: "Asclepius." Translated by James Brashler, Peter A. Dirkse, and Douglas M. Parrott. In *The Other Bible*. Edited by Willis Barnstone. San Francisco: HarperSanFrancisco, 1984.

CHAPTER 1

Audette, John R. "The New Answers—A Meaning for This Life and the Next." In Laszlo, Ervin, *The Intelligence of the Cosmos: Why We Are Here*. Rochester, VT: Inner Traditions, 2017.

"The Hymn of the Pearl." In *The Other Bible*. Edited by Willis Barnstone. San Francisco: HarperSanFrancisco,1984.

Tolle, Eckhart. *The Power of Now*. Novato, CA: Namaste Publishing & New World Library, 1999.

Steindl-Rast, Brother David. "Learning to Die." *Parabola: The Search for Meaning,* February 29, 2016.

Krishnamurti, Jiddu. *Wholeness of Life*. New York: HarperCollins, 1981.

Campbell, Joseph with Bill Moyers. *The Power of Myth*. Edited by Betty Sue Flowers. New York: Doubleday, 1988.

Merton, Thomas. *No Man Is an Island*. Boston: Mariner Books, 2002.

Sri Aurobindo. *The Life Divine*. Pondicherry, India: Sri Aurobindo Trust, 1938–1940.

—. "Works of the Mother, Part Two." In *Living Within: The Yoga Approach to Psychological Health and Growth*. Pondicherry, India: Sri Aurobindo Ashram, 1987.

CHAPTER 2

LeLoup, Jean-Yves. *The Gospel of Mary Magdalene*. Rochester, VT: Inner Traditions International, 2002.

Rowling, J. K. *Harry Potter and the Prisoner of Azkaban*. New York: Scholastic Inc., 1999.

Deloria Jr., Vine. *God Is Red: A Native View of Religion*. Golden, CO: Fulcrum Publishing, 1994.

CHAPTER 3

Lama Surya Das. *Letting Go of the Person You Used to Be,* New York: Broadway Books, 2003.

Rinpoche, Nawang Gehlek. *Good Life, Good Death: Tibetan Wisdom on Reincarnation*. New York: Riverhead Books, 2001.

Humphreys, Christmas. *Western Approach to Zen*. Wheaton, IL: The Theosophical Publishing House, 1999.

Collins, Mabel. *Light on the Path and Through the Gates of Gold*. Pasadena, CA: Theosophical University Press, 1997.

Chödrön, Pema. *Start Where You Are*. New York: One Spirit, 1994.

CHAPTER 4

Freke, Timothy, and Peter Gandy. *The Laughing Jesus: Religious Lies and Gnostic Wisdom*. New York: Harmony Books, 2005.

Lachman, Gary. *A Secret History of Consciousness*. Great Barrington, MA: Lindisfarne Books, 2003.

Roberts, Jane. *The Nature of Personal Reality*. San Rafael, CA: Amber-Allen Publishers, 1974.

—. *The Seth Material*. San Rafael, CA: Amber-Allen Publishers, 1974.

Wallace, B. Alan. "Awakening to the Dream." *Tricycle: The Buddhist Review*, Winter 2006.

Dalai Lama. *Sleeping, Dreaming, and Dying: An Exploration of Consciousness*. Somerville, MA: Wisdom Publications, 1997.

Thurman, Robert. *The Jewel Tree of Tibet: The Enlightenment Engine of Tibetan Buddhism*. New York: Free Press, 2005.

CHAPTER 5

Newberg, Andrew, in an interview for the Summer 2005 issue of *EnlightenNext*, "Who Are You? Science's Quest to Solve the Mystery of Consciousness."

Wilber, Ken. *The Spectrum of Consciousness*. Wheaton, IL: The Theosophical Publishing House, 1993.

Goswami, Amit. *Physics of the Soul: The Quantum Book of Living, Dying, Reincarnation, and Immortality*. Charlottesville, VA: Hampton Roads Publishing Company, 2001.

Laszlo, Ervin. *Science and the Akashic Field: An Integral Theory of Everything*. Rochester, VT: Inner Traditions International, 2004.

Hameroff, Stuart. Quoting Cohon, Rabbi Samuel M., in *The Origins of Awareness*, a talk given for Yom Kippur 5761 at the Center for Consciousness Studies at the University of Arizona's annual Science of Consciousness conference, 2001.

Blavatsky, Helena Petrovna. *The Secret Doctrine*. Wheaton, IL: Theosophical Publishing House, 1993.

Goswami, Amit. *The Self-Aware Universe*. New York: Jeremy P. Tarcher/ Putnam, 1993.

Heidegger, Martin R. *Being and Time*. New York: Harper Perennial Modern Classics, 2008.

Mead, G.R.S. *Echoes from the Gnosis*. Wheaton, IL: The Theosophical Publishing House, 2006.

CHAPTER 6

Holmes, Ernest. *The Science of Mind*. New York: Jeremy P. Tarcher/ Putnam, 1938.

Eddington, Arthur Stanley. *The Nature of the Physical World*. Whitefish, MT: Kessinger Publishing LLC, 2010.

Hodgkinson, Brian. *The Essence of Vedanta*. London: Arcturus Publishing Ltd., 2006.

Kaplan, Aryeh. *Sefer Yetzirah: The Book of Creation*. Boston: Red Wheel/Weiser, LLC, 1997.

CHAPTER 7

Ripman, Hugh Brockwell. "Questions and Answers Along the Way." *Parabola: The Search for Meaning*, Summer 2011.

Rosenblum, Bruce, and Fred Kuttner. *Quantum Enigma*. New York: Oxford University Press, 2006.

CHAPTER 8

Ravindra, Ravi. "Freedom from Self: A Study of the Yoga Sutras," Parts 1–4. YouTube webinar from the Theosophical Society in America, Wheaton, IL, December 6, 2017. theosophy.world/ freedom-self-study-yoga-sutras-ravi-ravindra.

Mitchell, Stephen, trans. *The Bhagavad Gita: A New Translation*. New York: Three Rivers Press, 2000.

CHAPTER 9

Csikszentimihalyi, Mihaly. *Flow: The Psychology of Optimal Experience*. New York: Harper & Row, 1990.

Lama Surya Das. *Letting Go of the Person You Used to Be*. New York: Broadway Books, 2003.

CHAPTER 10

McKay, Betsy. "U.S. Life Expectancy Declines Further." *Wall Street Journal*, November 29, 2018.

Eddy, Mary Baker. *Science and Health with Key to the Scriptures*. Boston: The First Church of Christ, Scientist, 1903.

Ravindra, Ravi. *Heart Without Measure*. Sandpoint, ID: Morning Light Press, 2004.

Ikeda, Daisaku, René Simard, and Guy Bourgeault. *On Being Human: Where Ethics, Medicine and Spirituality Converge*. Santa Monica, CA: Middle Way Press, 2003.

CHAPTER 11

Butler, Katy. *Knocking on Heaven's Door*. New York: Scribner Books, 2013.

Helliker, Kevin. "Denying Death No More." *Wall Street Journal*, October 21, 2003. wsj.com/articles/SB106616432463567000.

Arnst, Catherine. "Getting Rational about Rationing." *Businessweek*, November 17, 2003.

Bell, Michael. "Why 5% of Patients Create 50% of Health Care Costs." *Forbes*, January 10, 2013.

CHAPTER 12

Toews, Ann. "*Everything Happens for a Reason* and *Natural Causes* Review: The False God of 'Wellness.'" *Wall Street Journal*, May 22, 2018. wsj.com/articles/everything-happens-for-a-reason-and-natural-causes-review-the-false-god-of-wellness-1527029046.

Thich Nhat Hanh. *No Death, No Fear: Comforting Wisdom for Life.* New York: Riverhead Books, 2002.

CHAPTER 13

Storm, Howard. *My Descent into Death,* New York: Doubleday, 2005.

Albom, Mitch. *The Five People You Meet in Heaven.* New York: Hyperion Books, 2003.

CHAPTER 14

Haselhorst, Kevin, MD. *Wishes to Die For.* Scottsdale, AZ: Kevin Haselhorst, PC, 2014.

CHAPTER 15

Romm, James S., ed., trans. *How to Die: An Ancient Guide to the End of Life.* Princeton, NJ: Princeton University Press, 2018.

CHAPTER 16

Gibran, Kahlil. *The Prophet.* New York: Alfred A. Knopf, 1923.

CHAPTER 17

Eck, Diana L. "The Last Sacrifice." *Parabola: The Search for Meaning,* Spring 1995.

Rinpoche, Sogyal. *The Tibetan Book of Living and Dying.* San Francisco: HarperSanFrancisco, 1994.

Armstrong, Eileen. "Death: Leaving Home or Going Home?" London: *InSight Magazine,* the Theosophical Society, 2002.

CHAPTER 18

Watts, Alan. *The Way of Zen.* New York: Vintage Books, 1989.

Sri Chinmoy. *Beyond Within.* Jamaica, NY: Agni Press, 1988.

ABOUT THE AUTHOR

 Clare Goldsberry has studied religion since childhood. Her studies have taken her from Protestant Christianity to Mormonism, to the Ageless Wisdom traditions, to Gnosticism, and to Hinduism and Buddhism.

Goldsberry writes about religion and spiritual traditions for many publications, including *Quest* magazine, and her book *A Stranger in Zion: A Christian's Journey through the Heart of Utah Mormonism* won the Arizona Book Publishers Association's Glyph Award for Best Religion Book in 2003.

She has also published six books on marketing and sales strategies for small- to mid-sized manufacturers. In addition to being a contract writer for business and industry trade publications, she has operated a marketing and public relations business since 1989.

Goldsberry graduated *cum laude* from Arizona State University in 1991 with a BA in journalism and minors in marketing management and public relations. She lives in Arizona and has four children and two grandsons.